Checks at the End of the 20th Century... and Beyond!

(Accounts of my death have been greatly exaggerated!)

Published by The Green Sheet, Inc., Rohnert Park, CA.
P.O. Box 6008
Petaluma, CA 94955
(800) 757-4441

Published in the United States by The Green Sheet, Inc.

http://www.greensheet.com

ISBN 0-9670947-1-2

Cover design by Kathrun Parker

Text design by Julie O'Ryan-Dempsey

Layout by Laurie Ogg

Manufactured in the United States of America, R.R. Donnelley & Sons Company, Book Publishing Services.

First Edition: December 1999

10 9 8 7 6 5 4 3 2 1

Contents

Tables

Acknowledgments

I would like to make certain acknowledgments in connection with writing this book.

I wish to thank Julie O'Ryan-Dempsey, Suzanne Cagnassola, and Dr. Juanita Chamberlain for their significant contributions to this book. Julie's effort in book layout and design as well as the creation of detailed charts and graphs, make this book much more pleasing visually. Suzanne's superb data gathering efforts and meticulous review of the research material and sources have given me comfort in the quality of the data provided. And Juanita's constructive criticism and much needed editing makes this book much more readable, in spite of its technical nature.

I also wish to thank the National Organization of Clearing Houses for providing their information and for answering my endless questions.

In addition I wish to thank Bob Ficarra for pointing out to me that the void created by limited check payment data could be corrected, and to Timothy LaBadie for encouraging me to fill that void.

Finally, I wish to thank my wife, Tischa, for her continued good-natured patience and assistance.

Nothing of real value in my life has ever been accomplished without assistance from others and this has been no exception.

Foreword

This book needed to be written: first, to dispel the myth of the demise of the check; second, to provide a comprehensive reference resource for the work of others; and third, to offer a cultural commentary on the payment system in America at the end of the twentieth century.

Until now, no one has attempted to gather the check data scattered throughout the publications and reports of the financial services industry, organize it, analyze it, and present it with checks as the primary field of consideration. In most instances, financial services literature calls upon check data as supporting information for arguments dedicated to other subjects—and interpreted accordingly.

At present, there are no experts in the U.S. who have the definitive answer to the future of the paper check. There are only a few researchers who, like myself, have labored to discover the history of the check and the trends of check usage through the years, then recount their findings for others. Each of their reports or informed opinions depends both on information about the past, and on various levels of assumptions about the future.

In my informed opinion, checks show no signs of disappearing anytime soon. In fact, aided by a number of current trends, checks may continue to flourish for quite some time. One such trend in recent years is the increase in the practice of writing multiple checks for a single payment. Consumers often write several checks to pay separate portions of a bill; for example, the telephone bill. Furthermore, despite an increase in the use of ATMs and electronic payment methods, such as electronic funds transfer and debit cards, there has been no corresponding decrease in check volume. Against all predictions, check volume continues to increase.

Why do predictions fail? Most often, the answer is that something important has been left out of the calculation. In the chapters that follow, I will contend that the pundits who predict the demise of the check (often down to the very date) have left out two essential considerations: the consumer's strong interest in checks as a medium of payment and the continuing reliance of the nation's financial and commercial interests on the check.

Consumers like their checks for many reasons, and surveys reflect consumers' stubborn resistance to relinquishing the convenience, security, and universal acceptance of check payment. Moreover, the electronic alternatives to checks, on which the futuristic planners of the financial services industry count so heavily, have yet to close the gap between strategy and execution—and still have a long way to go before they do.

A long list of factors emerges from the available sources of check data, pointing both to the strength of consumer preference for checks and to the ongoing (albeit unrecognized) importance of the check to the financial and commercial interests of the U.S.—all of which, taken together, confirm a continuing growth in checks as the twentieth century comes to a close. As a sampling, here is the short list:

- 88% of the population, or 174 million, people have a checking account.
- 1% more females have checking accounts than males.
- Consumers prefer checks 4 to 1 against debit cards.
- In 1998 check printers printed 4.3% more checks than in 1997.
- 72% of consumers believe that their check use will increase or stay the same over the next year.
- Americans write an average of 25 checks per month.
- 60% of PC-initiated payments still end up as paper checks.
- As income rises, so does the use of checking accounts.
- During the last five years, the value of checks written has increased 25%.
- Checks represent 45.2% of all payments in the U.S.
- 53% of retailers are reporting continued check growth.
- The number of checks written will grow 1 to 2% a year for the next six to seven years.
- The total number of checks written by 2005 will be more than 73 billion.
- More than 6.3 billion new checks will come into the payment system between 1999 and 2005.
- The average check amount will grow to $855.12 in 2005.
- Checks today account for more than 25% of U.S. Postal Service revenue.
- Banks earn more than $5.6 billion a year from bounced check fees.
- The value of check float to banks is worth more than the cost of check processing.
- Paper checks cost less than half the expense of processing payments electronically.
- The Federal Reserve banks clear only 25% of checks in the U.S.
- 28 Bankers Round Table banks (representing 61% of all bank assets in the U.S) are committed to moving to check truncation.
- 69% of all checks are drawn on banks other than the top 100 bank holding companies.

- 35% of check routing numbers assigned to credit unions cannot be used to deduct funds from the account using the ACH.
- Should ACH collection of checks take the place of paper settlement, banks will lose 16 cents a check in overnight interest.

At present, many of those whose task it is to define the future course of the financial services industry take for granted that checks are on their way out and will be replaced by electronic payment systems sooner or later. In my view, those who make immediate business decisions on this unexamined assumption do so at their own peril. If consumers have their way, the decline will occur later, rather than sooner.

Eventually, checks may decline in number, but this change is still far in the future. The rise or fall of checks will depend on the consumer more than any other factor. Therefore, no one presuming to predict the moment of the check's ultimate disappearance can afford to ignore the formidable influence of consumer demand.

History and Background

1

As the twentieth century comes to a close, most consumers in the U.S. continue to find the paper check as much a household staple as food and clothing, and considerably more enduring in their lives. While many financial fads have come and gone, the paper check has continued to be the non-cash payment method consumers and businesses alike most often utilize. In fact, the check has become so basic to Americans' financial thinking that most of us give little thought to checks as we use them. As a consequence, the paper check is often undervalued—even by those whose lives and businesses are check-dependant.

> *"Get ready for cashless, checkless living: For many people it's already here, lots of advantages-but it's scary, too".*
>
> *Changing Times*
> *October 1975*

For most of us the paper check seems to have been around forever, and from a U.S. perspective this is really true. The earliest known check on record was written in 1659 by a Mr. Dalboe for four hundred pounds to the London goldsmiths, Morris and Clayton. Shortly thereafter the idea of the check crossed the Atlantic and has existed here in one form or another ever since.

Checks were regularly used as a commercial payment method as early as the late eighteenth century. Initially used by merchants for local settlement, checks had gained general acceptance as a method of local exchange by the early nineteenth century. By 1840, almost all payments in cities, except for small retail transactions, were made by check.[1] The popularity and widespread use of checks led to a twenty-fold increase in the number of bank accounts by the 1850s.[2]

The first clearing house association opened in New York City in 1853, established for the purpose of daily settlement of net balances among its banks. Banks in other cities, encouraged by the effectiveness of that first association, established their own clearing house associations soon after. Rural America joined in the national check usage trend after 1900 when banks serving farmers expanded into rural areas. By the late nineteenth century, checks in the United States had already become a domi-

1 Benjamin J. Klebaner, *American Commercial Banking: A History*, 1990.

2 The 1859 annual report of the New York Superintendent of Banks provides the twentyfold estimate.

nant form of payment, with nearly 85% of the nation's business-to-business transactions conducted using paper checks by 1909. Household checking accounts became popular as the twentieth century progressed, and the volume of checks processed increased from 3.5 billion per year in 1939 to 13.0 billion per year in 1960 and will be more than 69 billion checks per year as the century comes to a close.

> *"There are no technical barriers to the spread of electronic funds transfer. It parallels all the work done by the check system, and does it better, more cheaply, faster, and at greater convenience to all users of the payments system".*
>
> *George W. Mitchell*
> *November 1973*

Use of paper checks for personal and business payments has grown steadily for more than 160 years, and my research suggests that it will continue to grow for at least another 10 to 15 years. The paper check payment system continues to function very well, and there is no basis for anticipating a checkless society as predicted by bankers in the early 1970s even by the year 2050.

According to the National Organization of Clearing Houses (NOCH), "...the check still represents an extremely safe and efficient payment instrument that continues to enjoy widespread and heavy usage."[3] Primary Payment Systems, a major consortium of banks and electronic funds transfer associations, places the check mechanism peaking in the year 2021, "...with checks continuing to be consumers' preferred method of payment."[4] In the 1996 ***Report of the Settlement Risk Management Task Force,*** the National Organization of Clearing Houses (NOCH) reports, "Processing conventions, technology, clearing options, and the law governing the check payment system have experienced significant

> *"Between 1987 and 1989, we expect personal check writing to reach its historic plateau for the twentieth century."*
>
> *Federal Reserve Bank of Atlanta, Economic Review, August 1983*

3 National Organization of Clearing Houses and the National Automated Clearing House Association, *Report of the Settlement Risk Management Task Force*, Migration Section, (Herndon, VA: published report, 1995), p. 22.

4 Primary Payment Systems, Inc. (PPS), chart "Projected Check Usage in the United States," 1995 Brochure (1995), p. 6. PPS is owned and controlled by Financial Institutions and EFT Networks, maintaining over 30 million checking accounts from 26 financial institutions primarily located in the Western United States, as noted in New York Clearing House, Primary Payment Systems, Inc. press release, *The Battle Against Check Fraud Gains Momentum through Powerful Alliance*, (May 14, 1996).

> *"The growth of check writing at the point of sale, projected at a rate of 2% a year by First Data Corp., runs counter to the trend of electronic commerce. And unless retailers begin refusing checks and banks discontinue issuing checking accounts—both of which are very unlikely soon—some consumers will continue to prefer paying with checks over other forms of payment."*
>
> *Chain Store Age*
> *October 1998*

development through the years, and today the check remains as one of the primary means of payment in the United States and internationally."[5]

For nearly three decades the banking industry has been trying to eliminate the paper check in favor of an electronic payment system. As the twenty-first century begins, banks are clearly improving the speed and security of check handling through electronic presentment strategies and bank automation, while hundreds of paperless pilot programs continue to explore new technology, strengthening the banking system's ability to achieve electronic settlement.

"Electronic check presentment, image technology, and bank-to-customer information links offer promising advancements that will ensure the continued life of the check as a primary means of payment well into the next century."[6] Although the Federal Reserve Board announced as early as 1971 that it intended to move with deliberate speed toward an electronic system, the number of paper checks has steadily increased during the ensuing 29 years, with no hint of a major decline.

In the 1970s, the number of paper checks was growing at an 8% annual level, which outpaced both the growth of the population and that of the economy. In the 1980s, check growth slowed to a 6% annual rate. In the 1990s, the growth rate has been approximately 3.6%. NOCH projected continuing growth at an annual rate greater than 1% into the next century.[7] My research suggests a growth rate of 1% or better through 2005, with dollar volume growth continuing to outpace transaction growth.

5 National Organization of Clearing Houses and the National Automated Clearing House Association, loc. cit.

6 Ibid., Conclusion, p. 22.

7 Ibid., The Check Collection Environment, p. 22.

Checks Today

2

In 1979, checks accounted for 11% of all payments. In 1999, twenty years later, checks still account for 10% of all payments and two-thirds of all banking system volume.

Overall checks exceed 68 billion items a year (see Table 10) with 31 billion checks written by businesses and the government and more than 37 billion checks written by consumers. The primary payee for individual consumer checks continues to be the business community, representing 87% of the total checks written by consumers. Consumers write between 33 and 35% of their total checks at the point-of-sale[8] and 52% from home for recurring bills. This means that checks accepted at retail create significant business for banks, including 12 to 14 billion in personal check deposits annually. The primary payee for business checks (57%)[9] is other businesses, while the primary payee for federal, state, and local government checks (78%) is individuals.

Today, checks passing through the U.S. mail system account for more than a quarter of Postal Service revenue. American consumers and businesses are writing checks worth 25% more than five years ago and 50% more than a decade ago. U.S. banks generate $60 billion from DDA accounts, and this heavily subsidizes the branch-banking network throughout the U.S.

More than 50% of bank revenues are from available balances, with $7 billion from NSF fees—all of which are at risk if the check disappears from the American landscape. In addition, according to Dr. Alan Lipis, Chief Executive of Global Concepts, one of the nation's best-known bank research and benchmarking firms, "The value of (check) float to banks is worth more than the total cost of check processing."[10]

Eighty-eight percent of U.S. adults (174 million people) have checking accounts. No other financial instrument or interaction claims acceptance and use with such a high percentage of the population. Checks support a large segment of this country's economy as well. Global Concepts estimates that the check as a payment system supports more than 244,500 jobs while still

8 Allen H. Lipis, "The Paper Check is Here to Stay-and That's Good News for Banks," *American Banker*, December 19, 1995. Also "N. Y. Clearing House Joins Fraud Data Base," *American Banker*, May 22, 1996, http://www.star-system.com/ppsifraud.html.

9 A 1998 survey by Thomas Register of American Manufacturers surveyed 2,040 businesses, who responded that 78.8% of all of their payments to other businesses were made by check.

10 Allen H. Lipis, Ph.D., "The Indelible Check," opening address, Check Payment Systems Association 47th Annual Meeting, April 19, 1999.

remaining a highly efficient system.[11] The total annual payroll of the employees in the checking industry is approximated to exceed $6.1 billion.

"Indeed, we appear to be the only industrial country in which the per capita number of checks written is still rising, despite rapid growth in payments by credit and debit cards or other electronic means."[12]

11 Corporate income taxes tied to the checking industry and paid by non-bank parties are estimated to be between $600 million and $1.25 billion each year. Global Concepts also surmises that employees and their employers in the checking industry contribute almost $917 million to Social Security each year while employees in the checking industry contribute more than $61 million to Medicare each year. Sales tax on printed checks totals over $200 million each year. Global Concepts estimates that employees devoted to and supported by the check contribute nearly $619 million in taxes to the Federal Government and $124 million in taxes to State and Local Governments each year. In addition to these societal benefits of the check, over a quarter of the United States Postal Service's operating revenue stems from mail related to the check. The check as a payment system is extremely valuable to the United States economy.

12 "Payments Systems in the Global Economy: Risks and Opportunities," May 1998, Federal Reserve Bank of Chicago, p. 27-31, Alice M. Rivlin, Vice Chair of the Board of Governors of the Federal Reserve System.

Check Volume Continues to Dominate

3

Among adult Americans, the most popular method of payment for a variety of purposes continues to be a paper check.[13] This is true not only in consumer payments to businesses, but in business-to-business transactions as well. The American love affair with checks, long thought to be based on "check float", has since been shown to be based on other factors, including simplicity, universal acceptance, convenience, control and above all else, low cost.[14]

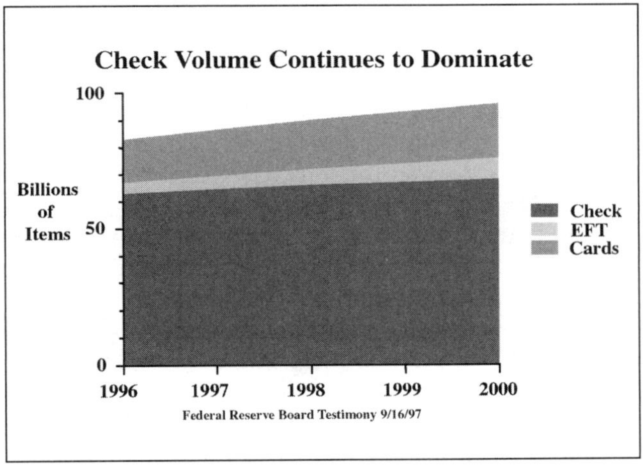

According to a 1997 survey conducted by Thomas Register for Visa U.S.A., the most popular payment method for business-to-business transactions was check, which received 78.8% of the survey votes. In 1998 the nation's check printers increased the total number of checks printed and distributed in the U.S. 3.6% over 1997 with a 4.3% "personal check" printing increase over 1997.[15] Since 1997, there has been a steady increase in the number of checks ordered for personal use, credit card convenience checking, and for opening new checking accounts. The total number of checks ordered has risen steadily from 38.6 billion in 1995 to more than 47 billion in 1998. Along with the number of checks printed, the 1998 check printers survey also showed an increase in the number of checks requested per order with the total number of checks ordered rising from 265 million in 1995 to more than 280 million in 1998.

In spite of all of these facts, in the late twentieth century an urban myth began to develop concerning checks. It became a "payments industry" belief that the paper check would soon be extinct. This belief has been highly popularized, particularly in

13 Opinion Research Corporation, Inc. (for Financial Stationers Association), *Payment Methods*, Summary Report, February 1997, p. 3.

14 Kirsten E. Wells, "Are Checks Overused?" *Federal Reserve Bank of Minneapolis Quarterly Review*, Vol. 20. No. 4, Fall 1996, pp. 2-12. In real terms, between 1987 and 1993, the value of float for an average check payment dropped from $1.04 to $0.09, or about 90%. The reasons for this dramatic drop in the value of float are primarily greater efficiency in check processing and lower short-term interest rates.

15 "1998 U.S. Check Shipment Survey Covering 1997 and 1998 Fiscal Years," Check Payment Systems Association, April 2, 1999, p 2. According to the CPSA report, 92% of the association members responded to the survey (representing 98% of personal checks printed in the U.S.), which was tabulated by an independent and neutral third party, Strategic Insights. The three major printers, Deluxe Corporation, John H. Harland Company and Clarke American Checks, Inc. were among the participants. The report reflects 45,446,494,489 total checks printed in 1997 and 47,077,953,064 in 1998.

the print media. For journalists the story of the demise of the paper check, with its consequent opportunity for speculating on both the replacement payment method and the date of the check's disappearance, promised an attention-getting human interest piece with which to fill the pages of daily papers and magazines. When NASA made space travel possible and computers became ubiquitous household appliances, many people reasoned that it was only appropriate for check payments to be "electronic" as well. In a nation caught up in doing everything faster, better, and more profitably, it just seemed self evident that there would be no place in the twenty-first century for the old-fashioned paper check.

From predictions by the Federal Reserve early in the 1970s that checks would never exceed 22 billion items per year, to a long line of would-be paper check replacements, including credit cards, online bill payments, ATMs, and debit cards, the paper check has survived attack after attack and still continues to grow. In the 1970s we were told that the check would be gone by 1980. In the 1980s we were told that the check would be gone by 1990. In the 1990s we now know that the check will not be gone by the end of the decade, and most Americans are hurrying to order checks imprinted with the date of the new century.

As the new millennium begins, it is becoming clear to an ever increasing number of payment system stakeholders that the paper check will continue to be around much longer than most of them ever considered possible—for reasons most never understood. The fact of the matter is that both businesses and consumers like checks, and they would find it hard to function in a world without them.

The Checkless Society:

1970s . . ."The Paper Check will be gone by 1980."

1980s . . . "The Paper Check will be gone by 1990."

1990s . . . "The Paper Check will NOT be gone by the year 2000."

Here's My Check. . .
***American Demographics*, March 1998**
(Projected billions of paper checks written in the U.S., (1985-2005)

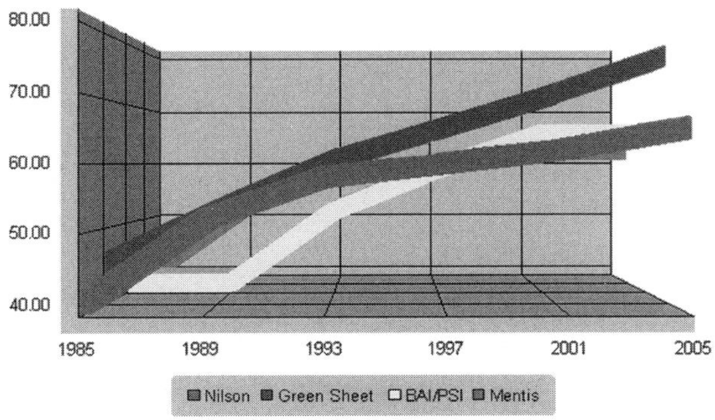

Differing forecasts for the number of checks that will change hands each year reflect different opinions on how rapidly consumers and businesses will adopt electronic payment options.

The longer the check has been around, the more the check system has improved; moreover, there remain many more opportunities to reduce the cost of this highly efficient system even further.

So why has the assumption that the check will soon be gone gained such unquestioning assent long before the reality of such an event is even remotely possible?

Understanding the Numbers

4

If checks could speak for themselves, they might well quote Mark Twain: "Accounts of my death have been greatly exaggerated." But checks can't speak for themselves, and very few people have ventured to speak for them, except in limited contexts, since check data is extremely difficult to pull together. For one thing—and this comes as a surprise to most people—there is no central authority on checks, no comprehensive body of check information that one might dial up, look up, or logon to.

No single source exists in the United States that tracks or reports national check information in a usable manner for check growth analysis purposes. Data must be gathered from the various sources that deal with individual segments of check clearing information and then must be analyzed and blended into a cohesive set of statistical data upon which transaction and dollar trends may be evaluated.

To further complicate research, much of the published data concerning checks is shot through with conjecture and extrapolation—not to mention intentionally misinterpreted by some payment stakeholders with much to gain from the movement of

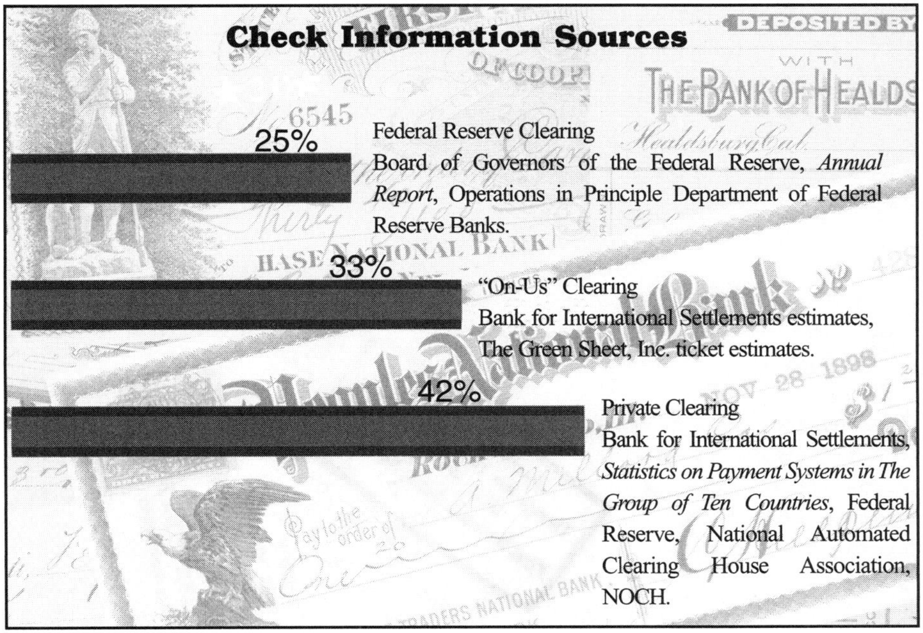

consumers from checks to competing payment methods. In the following chapters, I will review the available reporting sources for check data, including both published and unpublished material, as well as retail and consumer check survey information, and point the reader to the source of each.

Currently, checks in the U.S. are processed in one of three ways: first and largest in volume is settlement between banks utilizing private clearing efforts (42%); second is checks received by the bank on which they are drawn and referred to in the banking industry as "On-Us" items, as they do not get handled by any other bank (33%); and last is the check volume cleared through the Federal Reserve bank clearing system (25%).[16]

Non-Cash Transactions (per person per year)

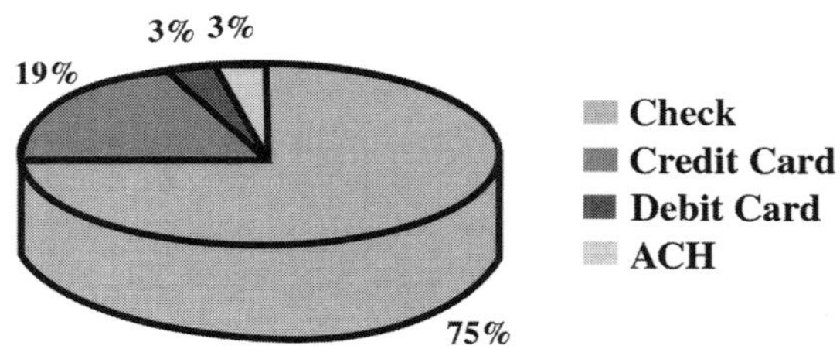

Source: Federal Reserve Bank of Chicago, May 1998 34th Annual Conference on Bank Structure and Competition

As check processing and settlement has moved from the central bank which once dominated the exchange of checks between drawee banks, to competing private clearing houses designed to make these exchanges more quickly and economically than the Federal Reserve banks, bank consolidation has also continued to increase "On-Us" item activity.[17] From year to year, these changing relationships within the banking community have obscured the check data, making it more difficult to piece together.

In addition, industry pundits have often regarded the paper check as an inferior payment product due both to the purported comparative costs of alternate electronic methods, and the much-publicized speed of competitive payment vehicle settlement. The relative value or veracity of these assertions of cost and speed aside, the fact is that for many, "paper" just isn't cool

16 Committee on Payment and Settlement Systems of the Central banks of the Group of Ten Countries, United States Section, "Payment instruction by selected payment systems: volume of transactions," (Basle, Switzerland, December, 1996), p. 107, table 8. Source data noted as U.S. Federal Reserve Banks. Also, National Organization of Clearing Houses and the National Automated Clearing House Association, loc,. cit.

17 Ever-growing numbers of checks are actually handled by the banks on which they are drawn, which also happen to be the bank of first deposit.

as part of a high-tech payments future. According to the champions of change, checks may have worked very well through the years for both consumers and retailers, but eTailers and cybershoppers can't be expected to take their checks with them into the twenty-first century.

While many payment system stakeholders would like to alter the way consumers pay for goods and services in a way that would be favorable to their own payment alternative, in my view, the most important part of any study of the U.S. paper check is what the consumers' needs and desires actually are regarding their choice of payment method. In fact, any speculation about the future of the check in our economy must also take into account the social and demographic changes that would need to come about for any significant reduction in the use of paper checks to take place in this country.

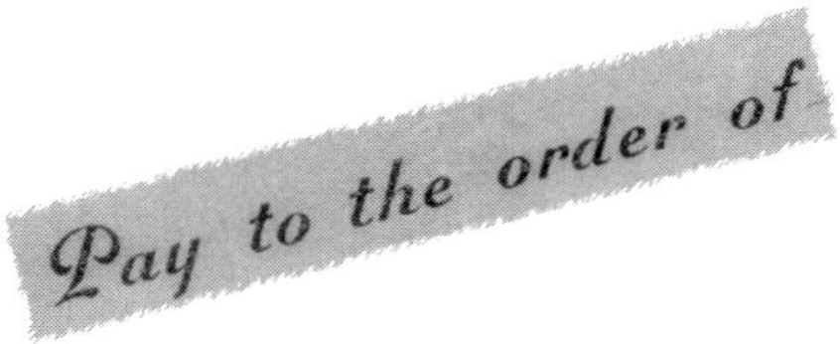

5

Consumer Payment Access

This study details both the difficulty of getting complete check information and reports the data available. The information about the number and dollar value of checks is of course, just informative data on trends and opinions. What we are actually dealing with in the question of the eventual demise of the paper check, is what the American public thinks about payment alternatives to the check, and if the alternatives are favorable, how long it will take to replace the check in any equally acceptable way.

To review consumer attitudes about the payment system generally, and about checks in particular, I initiated surveys in 1998 and 1999. As a starting place for this book I attempted to begin my consumer payments evaluation by reviewing survey information about who among the general population has checking accounts, and who does not. Our survey questions were designed to determine who had alternative payment access to debit cards, ATM cards and credit cards. I was also interested in the demographics patterns of each response.

Overall, two surveys reflected that 89% of the population have a checking account, while 36% have a debit card and 74% have a credit card. This information is the same as that reported by other survey results.[18] While these results are interesting in general, specific differences exist from the point of view of education, earnings, race, gender, age and region. One percent more females have checking accounts than males, with the greatest number of checkbooks as an example, carried by consumers who are ages 35 and older. As age declines, carrying a checkbook also declines, with the 18 to 24 year olds carrying a checkbook only 76% of the time. Regionally, consumers in the

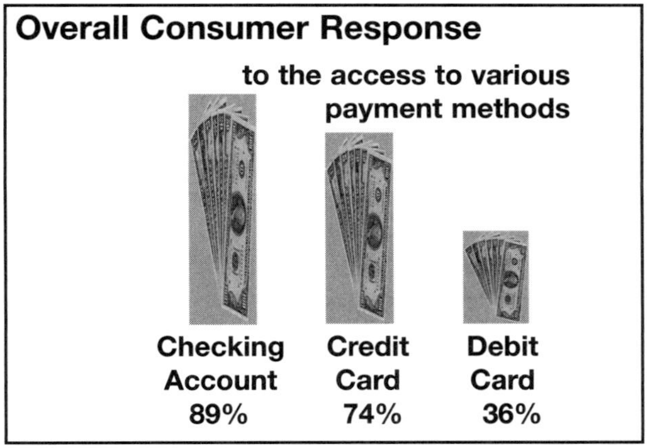

18 Shugoll Research, "Consumer Attitudes Toward the Concept/Process of Direct Deposit," *Automated Clearing House Payments: Market Research, Secondary Data Review, Prepared for Federal Reserve System*, May 1998, page 7, Section 2.3.1, "Consumer Attitudes." Report notes that Shugoll estimates that 13% of the U.S. population does not have a DDA transaction account.

Northeast and Central U.S. have checking accounts 2% more often than other regions of the country, with a 4% greater number of accounts (90%) in metro markets than in non-metro markets. In addition, we also learn from the survey results that, whites have the highest percentage of checking accounts (92%) with Hispanics at 83% and African Americans at 72%.

The correlation of income to access to a checking account tends to explain a number of other research elements. Consumers with incomes below $25K annually comprise the smallest survey population segment having a checking account. This segment has a checking account only 84% of the time. As income rises, so does the use of checking accounts. Ninety-six percent of all consumers who have annual incomes greater than $50K use a checking account. Differences in education levels of the consumers also affect the likelihood of their maintaining a checking account. At the low end of checking account holders are Non-High School graduates (75%), with college graduates at the high end (96%).

As a reinforcement of my survey numbers I also reviewed the demographic characteristics of the portion of the population the federal government had planned to convert from paper payments to electronic payments through the mandated program called EFT '99.

It remains my view that over time the elimination of checks at the federal level will likely result in creating more consumer checks in the marketplace, as a portion of the "Great Unbanked" will begin having their government payments electronically deposited into newly acquired checking accounts. These new accounts are the result of both the change in payment method by the federal government and the anticipated passing of legislation mandating lifeline banking services for the elderly and indigent, the primary recipients of such government payments.

Of the unbanked U.S. population who receive government payments, 3.2 million receive Supplemental Security Income (a program for the low income, elderly, and disabled), 4.5 million receive Social Security payments, and most of the remainder receive veterans' and railroad retirement benefits. The U.S. Treasury Department surveyed the impact of mandatory federal electronic payments and reported these survey results at a Bank Administration Institute conference in New Orleans in March 1998. While their consumer survey is limited to the individuals affected by the government mandate it tends to further support my survey data.

According to the Treasury's data, 52% of males had checking accounts, while 44% did not. Forty-seven percent of females reported that they had a checking account, while 56% noted that they did not. Of this sample of federal benefit check recipients, the mean age of those with checking accounts was 68 years old and the mean age of those without checking accounts was 62 years old. It is also interesting to note that the mean income of those with checking accounts was $29,500, while the mean income of those without checking accounts was $14,000. Finally the Treasury's data also reflected that the federal payment recipients who did not have checking accounts had a high school education less than 78% of the time. Interestingly, the Treasury's survey shows that 47% of those without checking accounts reported that the reason was that they don't have enough money to need an account. Among these families, 85% had incomes of less than $25,000.[19]

19 Arthur B. Kennickell, Martha Starr-McCluer, Annika E. Sundén, "Family Finances in the U.S.: Recent Evidence from the Survey of Consumer Finances," *Federal Reserve Bulletin*. January 1997, p. 7.

Since 1989 the number of consumers who do not have a checking account has been on the decline. In 1998 the number of consumers without a checking account was 11%, down from 13% in 1997, 15.1% in 1996, and 18.9% in 1989, according to a Federal Financial Management Services study.

While it may not be immediately apparent why strong negative feelings against receiving payments electronically, rather than physically, have a correlation with why consumers also wish to pay by check, a study by the Federal Reserve Bank of St. Louis queried 14 focus groups and 2,300 customers, businesses, and financial institutions about Automated Clearing House payments, and found that many consumers are concerned about losing control over their paychecks.

For example:

- What if they wanted to deposit a check over several accounts?

- How would they go about making a partial payment on a bill?

- What would they do if they needed to stop payment?

According to Kathy Paese, Assistant Vice President of the St. Louis Federal Reserve, "A lot of folks didn't understand how the process works. We're seeing clearly general confusion about how it works."

The St. Louis Federal Reserve survey also found that even if consumers had wanted direct payments, it just wasn't possible. Less than a third of the businesses surveyed offered direct deposit to their employees and only 13% of the companies allowed direct payments.

A similar study prepared for the Federal Reserve System by Shugoll Research noted that the problem isn't just about too few businesses making direct deposits available to employees. Non-users of direct deposit have very definite reasons for not doing so, according to the Shugoll research, and many of these reasons are grounded in a need for personal recognition and control. Some of the respondents to the study noted that they preferred to be paid by check because they like the feeling of being handed their paycheck. Also, there is a perception among consumers who do not like direct deposit that it is a threat to their privacy. They noted that they do not want their employers knowing their banking information or having access to it.

These same consumers have similar concerns about moving to electronic forms of bill paying, notes the Shugoll research. This too is about control. Consumers who want to hang on to their checkbooks indicated in the survey that they do not want to relinquish control over when their bills are paid or the amount of the payment. Electronic bill paying is expected to grow 150% by the year 2000, but it is not expected to make much of a dent in paper checks by then, even if 2.5 billion electronic bill payments are made per year by that point.

Because I was aware of popular assumption that the debit card is the greatest threat to the paper check, I also had questions asked about debit cards that could be correlated to checks. Coming back to the survey data gathered for this study, the 1998 consumer research showed that 36% of those surveyed had a debit card. Although this number is interesting, it is equally interesting that of those who do have access to a debit card only 25% had used the card within the seven days preceding either survey date.

Males and females equally hold debit cards, with the highest number of cards in the hands of the 18 to 34 year old age group. From age 35 on, the number of debit card holders declines steadily, representing only 15% of those 65 years of age or older. The largest numbers of debit cardholders are in the West (49%), 20% greater than the rest of the nation. Also, in the case of debit use in metro versus non-metro markets, debit cardholders are stronger by 13% in the metro markets. African Americans and Hispanics seem to have equal debit card access (33% have a debit card), while Whites have access to a debit card 3% more often.

As with checking account holders, debit card holders are most numerous at the $50K annual income level with 48% having a debit card, while only 24% have a debit card if their income is below $25K a year. Debit card to education data correlates with the checking account data, with only 14% of those who did not finish high school holding a debit card, compared with 44% of college graduates.

With clear differences reflected in debit card access for the low-to moderate income respondents, one can readily see why consumer groups are concerned that new check-replacement products may create a negative opportunity for banks and emerging payment processors to further segment and stratify the market for banking and payment services to the detriment of low-to moderate-income working families.

6

Consumer Payment Preference

Distinguishing a preference for using existing checking accounts or debit card, from simply having access to one or both may give us a clue to the consumer's perceived needs, which drive these payment preferences. Overall, the preferred payment method noted by consumers in both the 1998 and 1999 survey data is checks, receiving 37% of the payment preference response. This was followed by a preferred use of credit cards 12% of the time and debit cards 10% of the time. It is interesting that with overall access to debit cards and checking accounts being 2.5 to 1 in favor of checks, both surveys showed a 4 to 1 preference for check use. A preference for check use over other payment methods also varies by gender, age, and region. Females prefer checks as a payment method 42% of the time, while males prefer checks as a payment method only 34% of the time. Preferences for check use increases from 18% to 51% as the age of the consumer rises from 18 to 55 years of age. Regionally, checks are the preferred method of payment 42% of the time in the southern U.S., dropping to 32% in the western U.S.

Overall Consumer Use Preference

With access to checking accounts to debit cards at 2.5 to 1, consumer preference to use is actually nearly 4 to 1, and 42% greater than debit and credit combined.

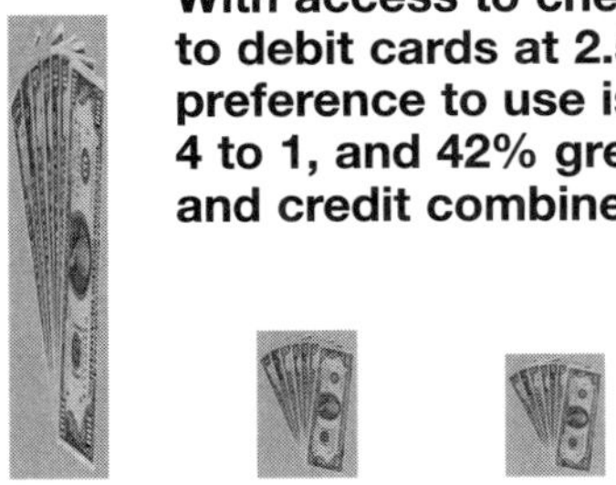

Checks 37% **Credit Cards 12%** **Debit Cards 10%**

Unlike the response to checks, males prefer to use debit cards 11% of the time, and females 8% of the time. The highest preference for payment by debit card is in the age group 25 to 34 years of age, with a preference for debit 15% of the time against a check preference of 27%—roughly 2 to1 in favor of checks. Furthermore, within this age group, debit card preference is concentrated in the portion of 25 to 34 year olds that is well educated and has at least a moderate income. Preference

Consumer responses to why a particular payment method is chosen:

Convenience or ease of access (53%)
Simplicity or ease of use (37%)
Acceptance (32%)
Float, or delayed posting (17%)
Don't know (11%)

for checks increases as the survey queries older, less affluent, or less educated segments of the population. The preference for checks over debit by nearly 2 to1 even in the segment of the survey population most favorable to debit speaks volumes about America's love affair with checks.

Differences Between Consumer Access and Consumer Use

7

The 1998 survey data reflects a slightly higher preference for checks over cash, however, according to respondents, their actual use of checks is much higher (20% greater) than cash. The highest actual use of checks is in the population over 55 years of age, declining as age declines. The highest use of both ATM and debit cards is in the age group 25 to 34, with actual check use exceeding cash, debit, and credit combined.

Concerning a respondent's sense of control over spending, when asked which payment methods are most helpful when budgeting 56% of the respondents choose checks over all other payment methods. On this same question, females chose checks 7% more often than males. Another interesting finding in both the 1998 and 1999 consumer surveys was the distribution of reasons consumers gave for using a particular payment method: first was convenience, second was simplicity, followed by acceptance and float. Eleven percent of the survey respondents did not choose any of these answers to explain why they use the payment methods that they do.

Asked their opinion of eliminating checks in favor of debit cards, 54% of those surveyed disliked the idea, 30% had no opinion, and 18% liked the idea. Over half of the respondents registered a dislike for the elimination of checks in favor of debit cards—a dislike females felt more strongly than males. As in virtually all areas of response, older respondents (55 or older) were more opposed to the elimination of checks than younger respondents. Among college graduates 58% were opposed to the elimination of checks, while 21% were in favor of the elimination of checks.

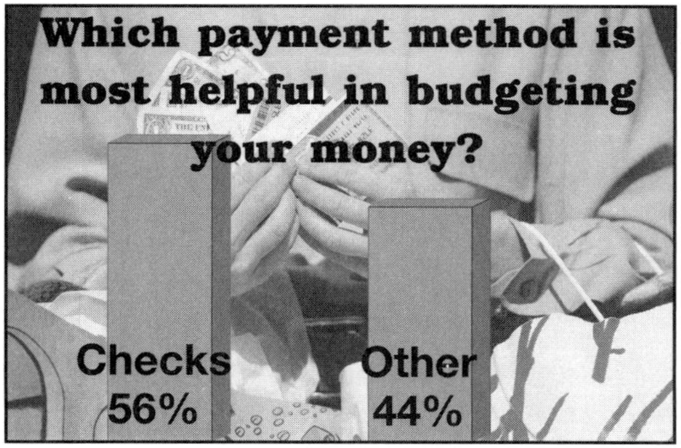

Asked whether they believed their check use in the next year would increase, decline, or stay the same, 65% of the 1998 survey respondents believed their check use would remain the same, while 10% thought their check use would increase, and 16% thought their check use would decline. Males responded more often that their check use would increase or stay the same than did females, and females responded more often that their check use would stay the same or decline.

Of the 75% of the respondents who believed their check use would stay the same or increase over the next year, those in the age group 18 to 24 noted this conclusion 61% of the time, while respondents 45 years of age and older noted this conclusion 79% of the time.

8

Most Recent Consumer Trends

All of the consumer preferences, trends, and groupings that emerged from the earlier survey work are further substantiated by the 1999 consumer survey conducted by Opinion Research Corporation International[20] at my request. The survey contained questions that addressed consumer opinions on the ever-expanding number of U.S. payment choices, as well as the consumer's planned and actual use of various payment methods.

What follows are summary results from some of the 1999 questions:

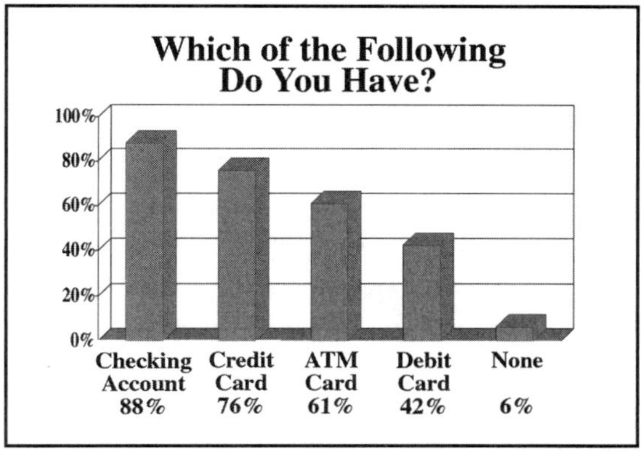

When consumers were asked, "Which of the following do you have?" 88% of the respondents answered "checking account",[21] 76% answered "credit card", 61% answered "ATM card", 42% answered "debit card", and 6% answered "none" in the February 1999 research. Answers from the previous year's research (April 1998) in which 89% of the respondents answered "checking account", 74% answered "credit card", 61% answered "ATM card", 36% answered "debit card", and 5% answered, "none" were not statistically significant compared to the 1999 survey, based on the sampling tolerances, with the exception of ATM card. The difference may actually signal a small increase in the number of consumers who now have an ATM card. (A respondent was free to choose as many answers as applied.)

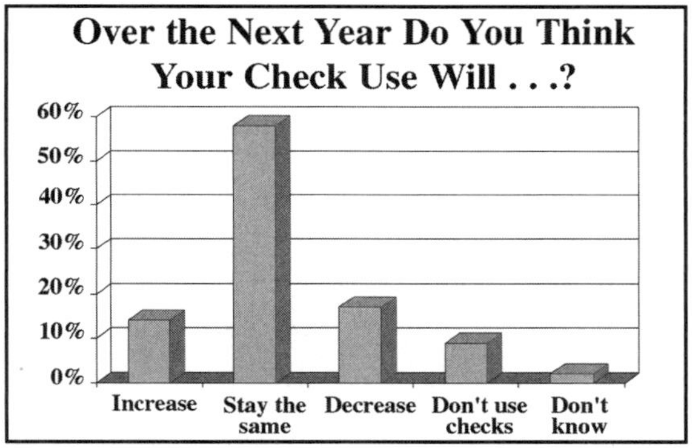

20 ORC International of Princeton, New Jersey, conducted a national probability sample of 1,009 adults comprised of 505 men and 504 women 18 years of age or older, living in private households in the continental United States. Interviewing for this CARAVAN Survey was completed during the period February 11-14, 1999, (Study #708078). ORC International conducted a national probability sample of 1,006 adults comprising 501 men and 505 women 18 years of age or older, living in private households in the continental United States. Interviewing for this CARAVAN Survey was completed during the period April 16-19, 1998, (ORC Study #70716). Completed interviews are weighted by four variables: age, sex, geographic region, and race, to ensure reliable and accurate representation of the total population 18 years of age and older.

21 Shugoll Research, loc. cit.

When consumers were asked in the February 1999 research, "Which payment method do you prefer?" 37% of respondents answered "checks," 33% answered "cash", 13% answered "credit cards", 11% answered "debit cards", 3% answered "ATM cards", and 1% answered "other".

In the April 1998 research, 38% of respondents answered "checks", 33% answered "cash", 12% answered "credit cards", 10% answered "debit cards", 4% answered "ATM cards", and 1% answered "other." In the February 1999 survey, by far the strongest preference for check use was apparent among older respondents. In the age group 18 to 24, 17% prefer to use checks as a payment method, 33% of those ages 25 to 34 prefer checks, 37% of those ages 35 to 44 prefer checks, 44% of the age group 45 to 54 prefer checks, 42% of those ages 55 to 64 prefer to use checks, and 46% of those beyond 65 years of age prefer to use checks. (The information by age has a 5% risk factor.)

72% of consumers believe that their check use will remain the same or increase over the next year.

In an effort to determine if there are any differences among access to a payment method, preference for a particular payment method, and the actual use of a payment method, we asked Opinion Research to query, "Which payment method do you actually use most often?" In the February 1999 results, 45% responded that they actually used checks most often, followed by 29% cash, 13% credit cards, 9% debit cards, and 2% ATM cards. In the April 1998 results, 47% responded that they actually used checks most often, followed by 27% cash, 12% credit cards, 8% debit cards, and 3% ATM cards. In this case, as with the previous two questions, the 1999 results were not statistically significant when compared to the previous year's answers.

I also asked Opinion Research to survey consumers thoughts on what the next year may hold for their check use. The survey asked, "Over the next year, do you think your check use will . . .?" In the February 1999 survey, 14% of the respondents replied that their check use will increase, 58% replied that their check use will stay the same, 17% replied that their check use will decrease, 9% responded that they do not use checks, and 2% responded that they don't know. When the same question was asked by Opinion Research in April 1998, 10% of the respondents replied that their check use will increase, 65% replied that check use will stay the same, 16% replied that check use will decrease, 6% responded that they do not use checks and 3% responded that they didn't know. Given the size of the samples for the two studies, and the level of response for checks remaining the same, 58% for February 1999 and 65% for April 1998, the difference is statistically significant and may mean that consumers are somewhat less sure in 1999 that their check use will remain the same in the near future.

From a consumer's perspective, the paper check provides one of the most important reasons—if not the only reason—to use a bank, as consumers continue to find an increasing number of ways to pay bills, borrow from non-bank entities, and handle their own investment needs. While the banking industry is keenly aware of the value of the consumer franchise which has developed around the paper check, banks are hard pressed to devise ways to reduce check cost, and at the same time, maintain the current level of fee income from check handling.

Evolving Check Initiatives

9

At the close of the twentieth century various check initiatives are underway championed by competing payment system stakeholders. In the case of banking, the key initiative is propelled by the belief that consumers value the information on checks and will continue to want the physical check, or at least a facsimile of it, returned to them each month. This has fostered heavy investments in the late 1990s in imaging technologies both on the part of some commercial banks, as well as all Federal Reserve banks, to return this perceived value to the consumer.

In 1995, 137 banks offered check images to their cash management clients. Among these were Bank of America, Fleet, Bank of Boston, Huntington Bancshares, Banc One, Harris Bank, Northern Trust, Signet, SouthTrust, Central Fidelity, First Chicago/NBD, Wachovia, and United Missouri Bank. Today, this number has doubled, with banks hoping the imaging service will enable them to keep old and win new customers, possibly generate greater revenue, and at the same time, reap operational savings as processes formerly performed manually are either shifted to the corporate customer or handled more efficiently by the bank.

The reason more banks haven't started offering imaging is that the technology is expensive. The up-front investment for a check imaging system for a large bank is around $2 million, for a smaller bank, $800,000. "What banks have to contend with is that imaging is perceived as a cost-reducing technology, and in fact, it isn't," says Dick Poje, partner at Treasury Strategies, Inc., Chicago. "It adds to costs. It also adds to the quality of work and throughput and a whole bunch of other benefits, but it comes at a price and until the corporate market is willing to accept that and pay for it, banks are going to be very reluctant to make that investment."

The fact that so many banks are willing to make that investment—ultimately a substantial investment in the paper check infrastructure—after three decades of attempting to eliminate the paper check in favor of a "paperless" electronic system well illustrates the dilemma at the heart of the decision-making process of the banking industry. On the one hand, DDA and checks represent 66% of banking revenue and 56% of banking profit. On the other hand, the banking industry doggedly maintains that the earliest possible truncation of checks, or even better, the wholesale elimination of checks in favor of an electronic alternate payment method, would save money.

It is nothing short of paradoxical, therefore, that image technology, electronic check presentment, and bank-to-customer information links offer promising advancements that instead of eliminating checks, appear to be lengthening the life of the check as a primary means of payment well into the next century, as electronics lower processing cost and speed information through the system. Today it is more apparent than ever that the bankers' primary goal, to reduce the banks' cost of handling checks, is achievable in numerous ways. (Of course, no plan to pass any part of these savings on to consumers is being discussed in the public arena.)

In its effort to streamline the check collection system, the Federal Reserve Bank system has led the way in the use of electronic check processing (ECP). ECP is a check collection process whereby a check is cleared based on information contained in an electronic file instead of the actual paper check (called the "physical item"). At a minimum, the file includes the account number and the dollar amount of the physical check. The physical check may or may not follow the electronic file. If the physical check is stopped before it reaches the paying bank (the checkwriter's bank that is, the bank holding the funds against which the check is drawn), the process is called "truncation."

The probability of check forgery will be higher with truncation, and the greater the check value, the larger the potential loss.

Those truncation initiatives that are being encouraged by the Federal Reserve banks are focused on retaining check information. They retain the check, but remove the paper from the system at the bank of first deposit. A competing initiative is designed to eliminate the check altogether, with check replacement at the point-of-sale and settlement through an alternative to the check-clearing system known as the Automated Clearing House system, or ACH. Only time will tell which of the two camps will emerge the winner of the "Check Electronification" wars.

Of the models in place, the point-of-sale model is the point of the most diversity and experimentation. In some market segments, retail initiatives seeking to eliminate the check and focus consumers on electronic debit of their DDA accounts are beginning to discuss point-of-sale imaging as a necessary element for long-term point-of-sale check conversion success. Check imaging would mitigate consumer resistance to changing payment types by linking the practice of eliminating the paper check at the point-of-sale with the banking initiative of imaging, thus giving the point-of-sale model a foot in each camp.[22]

Truncation, the bank initiative to take the paper check out of the system, can have paper to follow or no paper to follow. At the point-of-sale, however, the difference between check truncation and what point-of-sale initiatives call "check conversion" are imperceptible, making it easy to confuse the two. There are huge differences down the line, however—chief among them is "Who pays?"

ECP with Truncation: Weighted Average Per-Item Cost and Benefits, Compared to Paper Check Processing

Benefits/Costs (cents)	Additional Costs (cents)	Additional Benefits	Net
Depositing Customer	**.00**	**1.07**	**1.07**
Bank of First Deposit	**.14**	**.43**	**.29**
Intermediary	**.47**	**.71**	**.24**
Paying Bank	**.61**	**6.05**	**5.44**
Paying Customer	**4.65**	**.00**	**(4.65)**

22 The Electronification Alternatives Working Group of the Banking Industry Technology Secretariat of The Bankers Roundtable has established the following mission statement: The mission of the Electronification Alternatives Task Force is to *encourage the elimination of paper checks* from the payments process at the earliest possible point through Electronification; to encourage alternatives to replace paper from the payments process; and to seek, whenever possible, to consolidate back-end payments systems in order to eliminate redundancies and leverage banking-industry entities.

Truncation could be widespread, and few of us would be aware of its existence, whereas conversion transactions could grow rapidly at the point-of-sale, with banks enjoying a decline in paper costs, while merchants accept the burden of investing in conversion equipment. Of course, the truncation initiatives that are being encouraged by the Federal Reserve banks are focused on retaining check information rather than changing payment types, as in the ACH conversion model.

Under the current paper check practice, the depositary bank bears the cost of processing checks through an intermediary (if there is one) and of transporting checks to the paying bank. If the paying bank chooses to have its checks truncated by a Reserve bank (the Federal Reserve truncated 417 million checks during 1996) the paying bank has to bear the cost of truncation.

Those costs are directly or indirectly transferred to check-writers. Therefore, not only do payors have to give up their canceled checks, they are also liable for any other costs that will increase. In other words, voluntary truncation adoption might well end up redistributing any savings it produces, and it is unlikely that it will be to consumers.

Nonetheless, in banking circles, truncation hopes are kept very much alive, although—considering the poor record of some of the truncation pilot programs launched in the name of cost savings (to banks) and improved funds availability (to banks)——somewhat artificially, by regular infusions of the rhetoric of electronification and sheer enthusiasm.

In April, 1999, Michael Paiecki, chair of the Banking Industry Technology Secretariat (BITS), announced that 28 Bankers Roundtable banks, representing 61% of all bank assets in the U.S., have committed to the ECP (bank truncation) initiative by the end of 2000. While this may seem a significant foothold for this initiative, we must remember that the largest banks in the U.S. are only responsible for 26% of check transaction volume. While it is commonly assumed that it will take only a few banks to reshape the future of the check, this could not be further from the truth. Only 11% of checks are written on the ten largest bank holding companies in the U.S., and in turn these banks clear only 16% of the checks of others. In fact, 69% of all checks written are drawn on banks other than the top 100 bank holding companies in the U.S., and institutions other than the top 100 are the collecting bank for 54% of all checks cleared. [23]

23 Alice M. Rivlin (Committee Chair), *Committee on the Federal Reserve in the Payments Mechanism*, January 1998, p. 15.

Banks currently involved in check truncation and safekeeping pilots note that chief among consumer-relations issues is convincing bill-payers (check-writing consumers) that they do not need to see their cancelled checks. A number of bankers think this can be addressed in one of two ways: positive-response incentives, such as slightly lower cost; or negative-reinforcement incentives, such as adding a hefty surcharge for getting checks returned.

From the consumers' point of view, such incentives rather miss the point. For one thing, the consumer does not so much want to "see" the check as to have the check in hand in case it is called into question. For another, the consumer does not consider the check-to-payee transaction complete until the check returns, bearing the endorsements and bank verifications that declare the payment accomplished, to whom, by whom, and on what date. It is even a source of consumer resentment that banks now consider this final step, formerly an integral part of the package, an extra (and unnecessary) service.

My sense is that check truncation, the INFOBAHN solution to the "Checkless Society", will never get off the ground nationally in any meaningful way, as long as bankers and ACH executives are allowed to burden the process with arbitrary rules and procedural requirements. And even more important: as long as the process disregards the real-world concerns of the consumer.

One need only look at what happened with check safekeeping pilot programs when the National ACH Association became involved. A check safekeeping (truncations by another name) pilot launched by NACHA (National Automated Clearing House Association a Herndon, Virginia based trade association for the automated clearinghouse network) in late 1991 failed to generate any significant interest from either the corporate or banking communities. According to NACHA, after three years (late 1994), only about 100,000 checks a year were being converted to electronic form under this pilot program.

It is also now clear that any savings which can be expected from the elimination of the transportation of paper checks can be accomplished as well between banks, the proof being that the Federal Reserve cleared 13% of its check volume in 1997 electronically, and is expecting to reach 20% by the end of 2000. In short, cost is being taken out of the paper system without taking paper checks out of the lives of businesses or consumers.

William Osterberg and James Thomson observe in a February 1998 Federal Reserve Bank of Cleveland publication: "Although tremendous advances in computing and telecommunications have facilitated development of inexpensive, safe, electronic retail payments, neither the number nor the dollar volume of paper-based transactions has dropped appreciably. Moreover, only modest declines in the growth rate of paper payments are predicted in the near term".[24] In addition, the anticipated increase in the speed of check clearing by point-of-sale check conversion is limited at best, given the fact that most checks are already cleared overnight in the current paper environment. This means that only 10% of checks can be speed up with point-of-sale check conversion to ACH.

24 William P. Osterberg and James B. Thomson, "Network Externalities: The Catch-22 of Retail Payments Innovations", *Federal Reserve Bank of Cleveland Economic Commentary*, February 1998, p. 1.

Any long-term success of this idea is going to depend upon finding solutions to the daily balancing problems of merchants, on keeping investment in equipment to a minimum, and on doing a good job of accommodating the consumers whose payments do not clear or cannot be collected through the ACH. It is true that certain checks will always be problematic, and merchants must accept that they will not be able to clear every check through the ACH. Not all ABA numbers are ACH compatible, and it will take great expertise to make the process viable. With 29,000 active transit and routing numbers and thirty numbers being retired and issued every month, working toward a perfect point-of-sale check conversion system will require aggressive management—especially since the Fed has a backlog of some 5,000 numbers which it is still processing for ACH after their retirement.

> **Electronic Check Presentment**
>
> The obstacles include: Transaction costs, external network issues, uneven distribution of savings, an interim period of dual check processing, and the uncertainty surrounding check or image retrieval by the paying bank. And, if truncation is to occur earlier in the process, legal questions **abound** concerning consumer and banking rights and obligations.
>
> **Omitting consumer preferences from an analysis of the cost and benefits is likely to yield biased results.**
>
> Source: *New England Economic Review*, "A Comparison of Social Costs and Benefits of Paper Check Presentment and ECP with Truncation," Federal Reserve Bank of Boston, Joanne Stavins, Economist, July/August 1997.

The greatest stumbling block, however, is the fact that 35% of the routing numbers assigned to credit unions cannot be used for ACH, and 8% of savings and loans are not ACH capable. This puts the point-of-sale check conversion system—by definition an alternative payment system designed to obviate the conventional check-clearing system—in the strange position of having to devise an alternative to itself.

Ultimately, the situation requires that merchants subscribing to the point-of-sale check conversion system must have another system to fall back on. For the majority of retail merchants—certainly anyone who handles 10 or fewer checks per day—the practicality of dealing with two separate systems is doubtful.

As the truncation initiative to replace the paper check continues, so does the NACHA conversion initiative. Unlike truncation, which is driven by banking interests, conversion is an entrepreneurial venture, carried on by many individual businesses, large and small, that function at many levels of professionalism. The barriers to entry to this avenue of opportunity are virtually zero. Of course, each player is supposed to be working through a bank that has signed an agreement with NACHA to follow the rules. But the quality and stability of the services being offered varies so widely that I expect a fair number of these businesses to fail—leaving behind some very unhappy merchants. The question remains: will anyone's actions reflect badly enough on the conversion initiative to discredit it? The wonder is that it is already creating merchants who seem perfectly OK with the product—warts and all.

Despite the financial services industry's almost universal agreement that before the end of the twentieth century "electronification" of checks, which includes both truncation and conversion, would overtake and eclipse the paper check, and despite significant growth (in 1998 ACH activity was up 17.5% over the previous year, according to NACHA), the combined initiatives have failed to live up to expectations. Both truncation and conversion suffer from a host of problems which have, in practice, restricted the exponential escalation of their rate of adoption that was, in theory, so certain. The increased electronic activity, moreover, has not yet negatively impacted paper check growth.

Between 1987 and 1993, the average annual number of payments per capita increased 26 payments for electronic instruments, but by 31 payments for checks.[25] During 1996, 9.3% (approximately 1.4 billion items) of all checks presented to paying banks were presented electronically, an increase of nearly 40% over the 1995 level, yet paper check clearing continued to grow.

25 Kirsten E. Wells, loc. cit.

A key issue in evaluating the benefits of an electronic check collection system is whether it can be designed and implemented in a way that replicates the reliability, safety, and convenience of the current check system.

In addition, a number of legal issues also need to be addressed. For example: currently, the payor bank pays none of the cost of check collection, but has the legal right to insist on paper presentment. Other issues include the legal status of images and electronic payment records (for instance, on bank statements) as proof of payment both for commercial transactions and as documentation for federal and state tax authorities; the legal status of images and electronic payment records to prove that payment did not take place and that payment still has to be made; and whether the responsibility of verifying signatures should remain with the paying bank, or be shifted to the collecting bank.

Moreover, there remains the question of state laws that guarantee consumers the right to receive cancelled checks, either on an on-going basis or upon demand, and state laws and regulations requiring entities—such as trust attorneys or state treasurers—to retain actual canceled checks (as opposed to images) for auditing purposes.

10

Bogus Savings

In the financial services industry we hear discussions of new payment concepts almost daily, and speculations on the possibilities of the technological age that is now unfolding make a payment system far different from the one we use today seem inevitable in the not-too-distant future. A constant theme is that the way of the future calls banks-as-we-know-them into question. The threats to the present banking system are carefully enumerated: potential non-bank competition; the potential loss of a strong consumer franchise; consumer disenfranchisement; a major shift in revenue and profitability. It is on this final point that speculation touches ground zero, and the reality of the threat strikes home. For banks make a major part of their revenue and profit in the check segment:

Cash Management Revenue and Profit Distribution

	Percent of Revenue	Percent of Profit
DDA & Checking	66%	56%
Controlled Disbursements	3%	4%
Wholesale Lockbox	5%	8%
Retail Lockbox	3%	1%
Wires	10%	22%
ACH	3%	1%
ARP	3%	1%
Information Reporting	7%	7%

Currently, almost everyone in the financial services industry seems to be talking about moving away from checking accounts, and converting to debit payments or ACH or paperless electronic settlement in one form or another. Yet very little is said about how banks will replace the revenue that will be lost if these systems succeed in removing paper checks from the financial system.

The details are, of course, deliberately vague. There seems to be no consideration of whether companies and individuals will pay more to get less under check truncation programs, or if businesses which may initially pay lower fees for the return of point-of-sale checks converted to ACH than for their paper counterpart may end up paying more due to more returns and more presentments.

In an effort to create some leadership from within the Federal Reserve Bank in addressing the future of the paper check in the U. S., in October, 1996 Federal Reserve Chairman Alan Greenspan appointed a committee to examine the future role of the Federal Reserve in payment services. As 1998 began, the committee issued its report, the "Rivlin Report", named for the Vice-Chairperson, Alice M. Rivlin. The bottom line of the Rivlin Report is a recommendation that The Federal Reserve continue as a provider of both check collection services and (ACH) Automated Clearing House services, and that it should take an active role in enhancing efficiency, effectiveness, and convenience for all depository institutions.

The report goes on to provide additional recommendations whose implications reach much further and may not yield to clear interpretation. It recommends that the Federal Reserve banks should continue their current efforts to provide check truncation services to meet "market demands". But while it is clear that banks have good reason to process with both the Federal Reserve and private clearing houses as efficiently as possible (market demands), it is less clear whether consumers or even retailers are the demanders of truncation services.

The Federal Reserve should assess whether a coordinated move to POS Conversion or Truncation is feasible and cost effective.

The Rivlin Report also recommends that the Federal Reserve banks use their operational presence as major check collection intermediaries to facilitate the growth of point-of-sale conversion and truncation where "demand exists", but then actually seems to suggest creating the demand by recommending that the Federal Reserve price electronic check services to encourage the use of truncation and other electronic check services.

While some point-of-sale ECP proponents continue to argue that DDA/MICR mismatch or ability to get to the DDA is limited and controllable, the Rivlin Report goes on record that the Federal Reserve should address the technical ACH format and related issues that limit the ability of depository institutions and corporations to receive and to process vendor payment information.

The Federal Reserve's Report also includes the statement that it is not yet clear whether the whole check system would benefit from moving toward truncation. It recommends that the working groups studying this process assess whether a coordinated move to point-of-sale conversion or truncation is feasible and cost effective.

As the electronification of checks and other electronic money alternatives continue to expand, some industry pundits are beginning to question whether paper really is a more costly payment method than electronic settlement. In fact, it remains debatable whether the electronic alternatives will prove to be a cheaper solution. It seems self-evident to many who are attempting to devolve the payment mechanism to electronics from paper, that the ACH system is a cheaper clearing mechanism than paper. But as is often the case, this intuition turns out to be merely an unexamined assumption. The Federal reserve numbers do not support it.

The Federal Reserve system's Functional Cost Analysis, which was last completed in 1994, places the cost per ACH transaction at 14.6 cents for banks with deposits over $200 million. In the same report the cost of a transit check (that is, a check drawn on any bank other than the subject bank) is reported as also 14.6 cents.[26]

Some industry experts are of the opinion that the statement of equal cost actually understates the cost of electronic settlement. Allen Lipis, CEO of Global Concepts, an Atlanta-based payment system consulting company, which among other things provides benchmarking standards for banks says, "Paper checks cost less than half the expense of processing payments electronically. Additionally, the Federal Reserve Bank of Chicago

26 Joanna Stavins, "A Comparison of Social Costs and Benefits of Paper Check Presentment and ECP with Truncation," *New England Economic Review*, Federal Reserve Bank of Boston, July/August 1997, p. 32.

states, "Major banks in the U.S. process a check internally, excluding branch cost, for about 3 to 4 cents per item per bank, whereas the major banks process ACH items internally for about 6 to 8 cents per item."[27]

27 "Payments Systems in the Global Economy: Risks and Opportunities," May 1998, Federal Reserve Bank of Chicago, p. 167.

Check
Risk

11

Like so many other aspects of check information, check losses are difficult to determine due to the fact that such data is not maintained by any national reporting source. Although check losses at the retail point-of-sale are by far the largest check loss segment, a portion of this loss is reimbursed to some retailers by check guarantee providers, or is collected by the retailer on their own or through a third party collection organization. Annually, slightly more than 1%[28] of all checks written in the United States are dishonored, but nearly half of these are ultimately recovered, making payments by check one of the nation's lowest cost payment methods.

Payment Share of Personal Consumption Expenditures

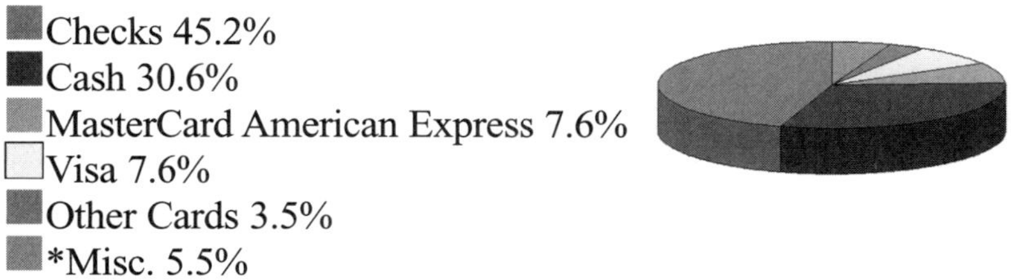

*Money Orders, Travelers Checks, Food Stamps, Preauthorization, Remote Payment

Source: 1996 Visa's Acquirers Workshop

28 Board of Governors of the Federal Reserve System, *Report to the Congress on Funds Availability Schedules and Check Fraud at Depository Institutions*, October 1996, p. 5, and Board of Directors of the Federal Reserve System, *Annual Report*, 1995. p. 303 (16,128 million items reported processed, 168 million checks returned. Calculation equals .0104166).

In addition to reporting and forecasting U.S. check growth, my research has determined that the segmentation of checks has remained relatively con-

Who Writes Checks?

Payor	% of all checks
Business	40%
Individual	55%
Government	5%
TOTAL	100%

stant over the last decade. Fifty-five percent of all checks are written by individuals, 40% by businesses, and 5% by federal, state and local governments. [29]

Checks represent 45.2% of all payments and 69.4% (75% according to the Federal Reserve Bank) of all non-cash payments in the U.S. It has often been discussed that of the 1% check problem, 10% is actually fraud while the balance is sloppy record keeping, slow paying consumers, dead-beats, and a large number of consumers shopping ahead of their paychecks.

In terms of all checks, 58% are relatively risk free. This percentage represents all government checks, business payments to government and individuals (principally payroll checks), and individual consumer checks drawn for purposes other than retail payments. As an example, the highest proportion of check losses in 1995 occurred for checks written by consumers against their personal accounts.[30] In terms of the highest risk checks, the primary risk associated with checks are for checks drawn for payments at the point-of-sale and business to business checks (see Table below). In spite of what may be perceived from the information above to be a rather stable national check loss history, in the survey reported by ***Stores Magazine*** in January 1997, responding merchants indicated their concerns

29 Federal Reserve Bank of Atlanta, "Displacing the Check," *Economic Review* (special issue), August 1983, p. 37. *The Nilson Report*, "Paper Checks in The United States," 1980-2005, published report, July 1985, reflects personal checks at 56.8%, business checks at 40.5% and federal, state and local government checks at 2.6%, with traveler's checks and money orders excluded from the federal, state, and local government numbers.

30 Board of Governors of the Federal Reserve, op. cit., p. 7.

Check Risk by Type of Transaction

Payor	to	Payee	Risk Level	% of All Checks
Business	**to**	**Business**	**High**	**23%**
Business	to	Government	Low	1%
Business	to	Individual	Low	16%
Individual	to	Business	Low	29%
Individual	**to**	**Business**	**High**	**19%**
Individual	to	Individual	Low	6%
Individual	to	Government	Low	1%
Government	to	Business	Low	1%
Government	to	Individual	Low	4%
Government	to	Government	Low	0%

over increasing check losses, with 64.7% responding that their stores had experienced an increase in bad checks over the past year.[31]

Check risk is managed in the United States in one of two ways: First, businesses determine which checks they will or will not accept, and subsequently attempt to collect those checks which are dishonored. These events may be supported through the use of individual or combined negative check writing history and through the use of third-party collection assistance, with the resulting costs and write-offs borne by the merchant. This risk management approach is called "verification and collection."

Alternately, businesses may contract for a third party to provide approval and guarantee services in which the third party has the collection and loss responsibilities for checks. The merchant pays a fee for such services. This risk management option is referred to as "guarantee." Given the risk management options, Ernst & Young found in their 1996 survey, that "one in four merchants avail themselves of third-party verification services to perform check authorization services. Another 16% say they use manual approval methods and 13.3% have established an in-house authorization system."[32] While historically, both verification and guarantee have addressed certain market needs, recently merchants were asked, "Do you feel the greater protection offered by check guarantee services justifies their additional cost?"[33] 64.7% of retailers responded "yes", guarantee justified its cost.

1998 Guarantee & Verification Check Penetration

Guarantee	**Value**	**Locations**
Top Five	$58B	395K
Other	$13B	205K
Total	$71B	600K
Verification		
Top Five	$285B	229K
Other	$41B	246K
Total	$326	475K
Overall	**$397B**	**1,075K**
	0.7%	**16.5%**

31 "Retailers See Rise in Bad Checks," *Stores Magazine* and The Reid System, January 1997. p. 41

32 *Chain Store Age* and Ernst & Young, *Survey Retail Payment Systems*, published report, January 1996/Section Two), p. 23A.

33 *Stores Magazine*, loc. cit.

My research indicates the fact that about 16% of all merchants in 1998 outsourced authorization or the responsibility for the check (guarantee), which represented less than 0.7% of the value of 1998 retail checks. Some 405,000 merchants with slightly more than 1,075,000 locations were outsourcing their authorization process or the risk of check loss during 1998 as reported by the various check guarantee and verification companies involved. I believe that this number is overstated in terms of merchant locations by about 10%, due to a level of sales puffing, as well as the fact that many merchants utilize more than one service, in particular, a verification service along with a guarantee service, resulting in merchant locations being double counted.

In addition, during 1998, the various check guarantee and verification companies in the industry handled some $397 billion in outsourced guarantee and verification dollar volume. I believe that the industry reported volume is also overstated by about 10%, for some of the same reasons noted above.

This means that verification organizations earned about $200 million providing negative data on $326 billion in checks, while guarantee organizations earned about $1 billion taking the financial risk on $71 billion in checks, earning five times the revenue on one-fifth the value of checks approved.

Elusive Fraud

12

According to Ed Lindsey, a detective in the bunco-forgery division of the Los Angeles Police Department, "Fake checks are out of control."

In California, the center of check counterfeiting activity, transactions involving fraudulent checks rose fivefold in 1995 at Wells Fargo Bank alone. However, this problem is not limited to California; Chemical Bank of New York also reported a 50% increase in fraudulent checks in the same timeframe.

The American Bankers Association says desktop publishing counterfeits are the number one crime problem facing banks. The proliferation of desktop publishing has created a new growth industry, the counterfeiting of virtually undetectable fraudulent checks. Banks and law enforcement officials say the cost to the economy could reach $1 billion a year by the end of the century.

According to proponents of both debit cards and point-of-sale check conversion, check fraud is a problem that continues to defy resolution. Despite the advent of new technologies, prod-

Check Fraud is on the Rise

Fraud cases involving amounts greater than $100,000

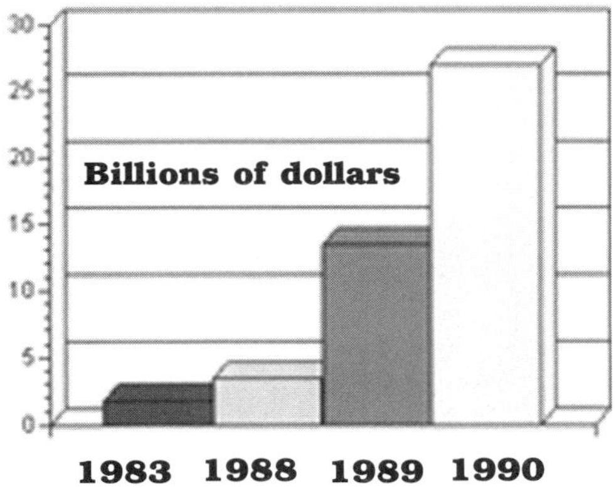

Source: Federal Bureau of Investigation

ucts, and services designed to thwart check fraud, companies that write checks and the banks that clear those items, continue to lose massive sums of money to fraud.

Bankers are particularly troubled by what they see as an increase in interest in desktop systems that are intended to be used by corporations to print checks in-house, complete with magnetic ink character recognition (MICR) lines. Desktop MICR printers can now be purchased for as little as $2,000.

Interesting Facts

How much money do U.S. banks earn from bounced check fees?

$5.6 Billion.

How much money is lost, annually, due to check fraud?

$600 Million

Sources: Consumer Federation of America and the Federal Reserve

On another note, proponents of the movement away from paper checks to check conversion and on to plastic debit vehicles, argue that fraud will be reduced or eliminated by either debit cards or their precursor point-of-sale check conversion. This, of course, assumes that fraud is a significant problem and not just bad checks or slow paying consumers categorized as "check fraud". William Roberds, a research officer in the macropolicy section of the Atlanta Federal Reserve's research department notes, "As is the case with currency, available statistics suggest that check fraud is not a large enough problem to significantly detract from the use of checks as a payments medium. The overall rate of check fraud loss is less than 2 basis points, or two-hundredths of 1 percent."[34]

According to a 1994 study by the American Bankers Association, 450 million checks are actually dishonored each year, which represents about 75 basis points of gross loss (.00746%) based on the 60,297 million check transactions in 1993. While I believe that this number was probably understated for 1993, it appears that the 1999 loss level was about 38%

34 William Roberds, "The Impact of Fraud on New Methods of Retail Payment", *Federal Reserve Bank of Atlanta Economic Review*, First Quarter 1998, p. 45. Estimates of the total cost of check fraud in the United States range as high as $10 billion annually. An extensive 1995 survey by the Federal Reserve found that banks' share of these losses amounted to $615 million in 1995. These "gross losses" do not incorporate any recoveries of lost funds.

As is the case with currency, available statistics suggest that check fraud is not a large enough problem to significantly detract from the use of checks as a payments medium. The overall rate of check fraud loss is less than 2 basis points, or two-hundredths of 1 percent.

greater. This represents a significant number of checks which will subsequently clear redeposit or will be collected through traditional collection means. Overall approximately 40% of the dishonored items will not be collected—only a portion of which are fraud items. The ABA's 1994 study notes that this amount is 1.3 million items or 3 tenths of 1 percent of the dishonored items, representing $850 million.[35]

A more recent study by the Federal Reserve put the number at $615 million lost by banks, thrifts, and credit unions on 529,000 fraudulent checks written in 1995. This same report notes that the Federal Reserve banks processed 168 million returned checks during 1995, and put check fraud loss at .001 percent (10 basis points) of the total value of all checks written that year (not to be confused with the number of items in the paragraph above). The Fed also noted that, based on the data available, the estimates of check-fraud losses for the years 1991, 1993, and 1995 are not statistically different from each other.[36]

All of these points aside, it is widely accepted that for some time to come, perhaps as much as a decade, the technology advancements needed to overcome MICR reader read errors, changes in banking rules, the creation of new ways to enhance or "scrub" the MICR data to cross-reference it to the bank accounts, and many other technical and legal problems, including placing at least another 4 to 5 million MICR readers at retail points-of-sale, will increase the level of checks that will not clear upon original presentment, rather than reduce them. It is fraud, however, which is only a small component of these dishonored checks, that is expected to be reduced by point-of-sale check conversion.

35 "Bounced Checks, Minimizing the Risk," *American Collector*, http://www.colector.com/pr/1997/97.01.10.html.

36 Board of Governors of the Federal Reserve System, *Report to Congress on Funds Availability Schedules and Check Fraud at Depository Institutions*, October 1996, pp. ii and 5.

It is a reasonable assumption that the future fraud problem for check conversion, particularly after it has realized its full anticipated success in changing consumer habits to some type of input or ID device (most likely a debit card), which is all the paper check is used for in the current point-of-sale check conversion processing model, will likely look much like credit card fraud. While conversion proponents believe that this future will represent lower fraud results, it is interesting to note that the current fraud associated with credit cards may be twice the level of the current fraud with paper checks.

According to Roberds, "The incidence of fraud in credit card purchases is quite small in absolute terms but is relatively high as compared with checks."[37] Given in the short-term higher returned checks, a U.S. installed merchant base that is only 25% complete in MICR readers, no tangible consumer benefits, a banking system that is on the verge of ringing out the last of the heavy expenses in the current paper system through truncation and perhaps greater fraud losses originating from conversion errors and conversion fraud, one must look to other reasons driving the forces of change toward the elimination of the paper check at the point-of-sale. Two of these forces are market share and bankers' fear that they will be disenfranchised from the consumer if they don't help eliminate the check.

First Data's alliance with Microsoft or other such non-bank bill-pay and payment-replacement alliances are often cited as the future of payments, as more and more Americans go online. In an article for the Bank Administration Institute, authors Neal Chambliss and David Taylor conclude, "Banking strategists will be sorely tempted to delay electronic payments ventures, which often have lower margins, so as to prolong the rich returns they now enjoy from paper-based operations."

37 Willam Roberds, loc. cit. While precise figures are unavailable for the credit card industry as a whole, one estimate put total (gross) fraud losses at $2 billion to $3 billion in 1993, and another placed this figure at $1.3 billion for 1995. Given aggregate credit card use of $879 billion for 1995, the estimates imply a fraud rate of between 10 and 20 basis points (0.1 to 0.2 percent). In the case of Visa and MasterCard, a study by the American Bankers Association (1996) estimated total gross fraud loss for 1995 at $790 million versus purchases of $451 billion, implying a loss rate of 18 basis points (0.18 percent).

Another Milestone

13

1999 marked a milestone in the social discourse devoted to the further possibilities of automating the clearing and handling systems associated with paper checks, as the electronics enthusiasts made a paradigmatic change in their "creative" thinking. Having achieved a higher level of technological consciousness, they scrapped the biological model on which the 1970s urban myth of the impending death of the check had been structured (the notion that everything comes to be, grows, flourishes, declines, and dies) and adopted a cosmic model: the new convergence mythology.

Along the lines of the latter-day prophecy that the sun, moon, and planets aligning in the sign of Taurus at the millennium ushers in a new life-cycle for planet earth, the payment system mystics have begun to tell the story of the "convergence" of check technology and need.

So the myth goes, the retail world has purchased MICR readers, the technology which has been utilized to read the magnetic characters as ID can just as easily use the same data for settlement, and both merchants and consumers want a better system. The convergence model dictates that when this many elements of a concept come together in such perfect alignment of capabilities and needs, movement in this direction is not only appropriate, but mandated. While these same convergence observers acknowledge that the current retail penetration and reliability of the equipment is significantly less than 100%, they believe that sheer demand will permit us, as a nation, to drag ourselves hobbling into this new era of "non-check" check acceptance at the point-of-sale.

While a number of imaging opportunities currently exist that would support reasonably priced imaging equipment at the point-of-sale, the investment necessary for manufacturers to build such equipment requires both venture capital and leadership, and are yet two more stumbling blocks to the realization of a hybrid check truncation and point-of-sale image electronic check system. As 1990s come to a close, it is nearly impossible to raise investment capital for anything check related. While it is true that little interest exists currently for anything that does not have a ".com" behind its name, it is also true that the volume of check activity and the value of the paper check system to society is completely absent from the minds of most venture capitalists.

As we go farther down the scale of affluence, what is being called a necessity is no longer a possibility or even a desire. The more affluent levels of society have little or no comprehension of the concerns of the less fortunate; therefore, they assume that if they have increased use of credit or debit payment vehicles at their disposal, and, for that matter, need not keep careful watch over the daily bank balance, the population at large enjoys the same privileges. But millions of others live week to week according to the latest balance in the family checkbook. Millions of others carry their net worth from day to day in a pocket or purse. The federal government recently tabled plans to pay benefits electronically. The reason is shockingly fundamental: there is no place to transmit many of the checks.

Discussing the financial circumstances that shape the daily lives of the non-credit users, the working poor, and the aging members of the U.S. population, a January 1999 editorial from ***The Dallas Morning News*** puts it this way: "The prospect of a paperless society and its promised efficiencies have been talked about for more years than most of us can remember. But this hurdle underscores just how vast a chasm exists between the working poor and the rest of America. Inadequate technology used to be the great challenge to electronic transfers. Now deeply rooted habits pose the biggest obstacle."

While Wall Street's movers and shakers have fueled the bank acquisition market, toyed with smart cards and securitized credit, reduced branch banking has been replaced by check cashing outlets ready and willing to meet the needs of the disenfranchised consumer who is left behind in the race to eliminate the paper check in favor of plastic. The future is with us, but it is very unevenly distributed.

Checks at Retail

14

While the Federal Reserve was experiencing an unprecedented 40% increase in electronic settlement in 1996, and Visa reporting 1996 debit card growth at 40%,[38] retailers were reporting continued check growth, with 3.6 million new checks coming into the marketplace each day (see Table 10.) In late 1996, retailers were asked the following leading question by ***Stores Magazine*** and The Reid System in an online survey[39] "Have your stores experienced a decline in check use over the past year?" with 52.9% of the merchants reporting that they had not had a decline in check use.

Respected organizations produce reports and research papers for various purposes. Each is based on what the researchers hope is a representative sample of consumers or retailers. Arthur Anderson & Co. surveyed 2,000 retailers in 1993 for their 1994 ***Survey of Retail Credit Trends***. Also, ***Chain Store Age*** and Ernst & Young combined two research studies from retailers and 1,000 consumers nationwide to form the basis of their 1996 ***Survey of Retail Payment Systems***.

Without exception, these studies report that checks continue to be a significant part of the overall payment system, representing 23 to 24% of retail sales. Checks represented 23.3% of all retail transactions in 1993, up from 20.5% in 1992, according to Arthur Anderson & Co. The value of checks also increased 29% for retailers who report annual sales in excess of $200 million.[40]

Research reflects the fact that consumers would often prefer to use checks even more than they currently do, as indicated by stronger consumer preferences expressed in surveys than the actual reported use by retailers (see Tables 1 through 3 on page 83).

38 CardFlash, "VISA Check Card Too Popular," April 29, 1997. Http://www.ramresearch.com/cardtrack/news/cf4_29a_97.html.

39 *Stores Magazine* "Retailers See Rise in Bad Checks," January 1997, page 41.

40 *Chain Store Age Executive* and Arthur Anderson & Co. SC, *The Fourth Annual Survey of Retail Credit Trends*, Arthur Anderson & Co. SC, (published report, January 1994/Section Two), p. 5A.

In fact, consumers surveyed in recent years have shown strong preferences for checks, as well as a desire to reduce their use of credit payment vehicles in favor of checks.[41] ***Chain Store Age***, a trade publication for retail executives, notes in January 1996, "Nearly 20% of household disposable income each month is now dedicated to reduction of credit card debts, the highest level since 1990."

In general, whether checks account for a larger or smaller portion of a business' total sales depends, for the most part, on the level of cash payment alternatives offered by the retailer. As Table 3 illustrates (see next page), checks at specialty apparel retailers represent about 20% of all sales transactions while checks represent 10% of transactions in department stores, 23% in discount stores, 40% in supermarkets, 11% in convenience stores and 26% in specialty non-apparel.[42]

Finally, in September, 1995 the American Research Group, based in South Carolina, contacted 1,000 consumers representing a cross-section of Americans on behalf of ***Chain Store Age*** and Ernst & Young. When asked about future payment options, consumers responded 75.1% of the time that they would expect their check use to stay the same or increase.[43] It is worth noting that the 1997 and 1998 ***Green Sheet*** consumer surveys received a virtually identical response on this important point as reported by this 1994 Ernst & Young consumer survey, while the 1999 survey reflected 72%. Again, these four separate surveys conducted over a five-year span are not statistically different in their response.

41 *Chain Store Age* and Ernst & Young, op. cit., p. 11A.

42 *Chain Store Age Executive* and Deloitte & Touche LLP, The Fifth Annual Survey of Retail Credit Trends, (published report, January 1995/Section Two), p. 6A.

43 *Chain Store Age* and Ernst & Young, op. cit., p. 7A.

Table 1
Consumer Check Preference as a Percentage of All Retail Payment Methods

Consumer Survey	Specialty Apparel	Department Store	Discount Store	Supermarket	Convenience Store	Specialty Non-Apparel
Ernst & Young	27.6%	22.1%	26.5%	36.6%	6.4%	26.2%

Table 2
Consumer Check Usage as a Percentage of All Retail Payment Methods

Retailer Survey	Total	Specialty Apparel	Department Store	Discount Store	Supermarket	Convenience Store	Specialty Non-Apparel
Arthur Anderson & Co. SC	23.3%	17.0%	12.0%	28.0%	40.0%	11.0%	26.0%
Deloitte & Touche LLP	24.1%	22.2%	7.5%	19.0%	39.2%		26.2%
Average	23.7%	19.6%	9.8%	23.5%	39.6%	11.0%	26.1%

Table 3
Consumers Whose Check Preference Needs are Not Met

	Specialty Apparel	Department Store	Discount Store	Specialty Non-Apparel
Prefer to use Checks	27.6%	22.1%	26.5%	26.2%
Actually use Checks	19.6%	9.8%	23.5%	26.1%
Lost percentage	8.0%	12.3%	3.0%	.1%

What does all this data tell us?

15

As I have noted earlier, there is no industry expert or final authority who has the definitive answer to the future of the paper check. Each report or predication, including the ones in this study, depends on both information from the past and various levels of assumptions about the future. The fact is, only a small number of people in this country are focused on the potential cost or negative impact of the check's anticipated decline or replacement, regardless of whether it is forced or natural.

For the foreseeable future, check volume is likely to remain at current levels or higher, despite the growth of check alternatives. Electronic payments will have to grow at astounding rates to overtake and replace the more than three-quarters of a billion annual increase in check volume. ACH, credit card, and debit card payments would have to double their current double-digit growth rates simply to stall check growth. While the Check Payment Systems Association does not foresee a decline in check volume over the next few years, even if the check were to decline in volume, overall annual check volume will still be in the range of 50 to 60 billion checks per year for years to come, even under the most drastic forecast of declining check volumes.

All the evidence points to the check flourishing for some time to come. In 1998, 87.7% of all checks printed by check printers were personal checks; 12.3% were business checks. These numbers reflect a decline in the printing of business checks as businesses increasingly use electronic payments and even create their own checks. Even though business checks have begun to decline, the number of checks overall has continued to increase.[44] Furthermore, while the use of ATMs and electronic payment methods such as funds transfers and debit cards has increased each year, check volume has not dwindled, but has actually increased.

"Despite repeated predictions of their downfall, checks continue to be written in the United States in ever-growing numbers, research indicates.

Estimated yearly volumes range from 65 billion to 70 billion items.

That makes checks and their longevity factors to be reckoned with even as the banking industry introduces more and more electronic innovations into the payment system. Yet even with the market research and other assumptions being made, it is difficult to pinpoint the size of the checking business or the timing of its long-anticipated decline. Fed volume rose 3.9% between 1997 and 1998. Through the first five months of 1999 the year-over-year rate of increase was 5.2%.

"There are a lot of decisions, policies, and assumptions being made by folks in the banking industry that are based on inadequate knowledge about the true economics of checks," said Steve Ledford, senior vice president of Global Concepts, a firm that has continually urged bankers to keep their faith in checks and their profitability.

"Banks make a good deal of money on the check," Mr. Ledford said. "It is a popular product, and the cornerstone of the bank-consumer relationship."

American Banker
August 18, 1999

The widespread use of paper checks continues to confirm the viability of the national check clearing and collection infrastructure as well as the consumer's continuing love affair with checks. While we often read about the imminent demise of the paper check because of the rise of replacement products such as electronic bill pay, debit cards, and point-of-sale check conversion to ACH processing, widespread consumer acceptance of these potential alternatives is still a long way off, and more people are beginning to realize it. "Electronic commerce has been one of the most overhyped businesses," said Robert Djurdjevic president of Annex Research in Phoenix. "The biggest benefactors so far have been the ad agencies." Alan Goldstein, staff writer of ***The Dallas Morning News*** writing in August 1998 notes, "For all the talk in recent years about electronic commerce, blizzards of paper bills and checks are still the norm."

This is not to say that it is not sometimes difficult to find positive statements about paper checks in a banking and payment system marketplace that is hot on the elimination of paper, yet some real-world statements still find their way through the scream of electronic is cheaper or debit cards are like checks, but better messages. The truth is that check-writing is still going up. "It is continuing to go up and has never gone down," says John Hall, spokesman for the American Bankers Association. "People are very comfortable with using checks, and to switch to some other form of banking makes them uncomfortable," says Donald J. Mullineaux, banking professor at the University of Kentucky. "Our volume of checks continues to go up. It's something we talk about, but we don't seem to be able to do anything about," notes Steve Kelly, senior vice president of Central Bank & Trust Co., in Lexington, Kentucky.

America's long-standing love affair with checks is still strong. Americans continue to write an average of 25 checks a month, 10 to 12 of which are for bill paying,[45] and the balance usually to acquire cash and to make retail purchases. According to the National Organization of Clearing Houses (NOCH), "...the check still represents an extremely safe and efficient payment instrument that continues to enjoy widespread and heavy usage."[46] In a 1998 report from the Federal Reserve Bank of

44 Check Payment Systems Association, "1998 U.S. Check Shipment Survey Covering 1997 and 1998 Fiscal Years," April 2, 1999, p. 2.

45 Longo, Tracey, "The Check is in the Ether" *Kiplinger's Personal Finance Magazine*, April 1995, p. 79.

46 National Organization of Clearing Houses and the National Automated Clearing House Association, *Report of the Settlement Risk Management Task Force*, Migration Section, (Herndon, VA: published report, 1996), p. 22.

Atlanta, the Fed concludes its 16-page booklet on checks saying, "Although use of automated teller machines and electronic payments methods, such as funds transfers and debit cards, have been growing each year, check volume has not declined but has actually increased slightly."[47]

47 Federal Reserve Bank of Atlanta, "The Future of Checks," *Checkbooklet*, 1998, p. 16.

Predicting the Near-Term Future

16

After reviewing the data, I predict continued check growth of 2% a year, declining to just under 1% a year for the next six to seven years, with more than 6.3 billion new checks (8.7%) coming into the system between 1999 and 2005. During the same period, I predict the value of checks will grow at least $6.9 trillion. While check processing growth continues to be questioned, the nation's check printing data confirms what the Federal Reserve and Private Clearing Houses already know, that the number of checks mailed to our homes and businesses during 1998 still grew more than 3.5%.

> *Paper checks exist in a unique evolutionary cul de sac. They and lawyers are the most survivable entities in the universe. In 2008 we will still be paying lawyers with checks.*
>
> *Thorton May*
> *Corporate Futurist*

Like it or not, from consumer surveys to check processing trends, it is clear that the paper check is going to be a vital part of the nation's future for some time to come. Check electronification initiatives continue to attempt to take cost out of the paper system while simultaneously planning the check's demise. Only time will tell if ACH proponents will win with their Check Conversion strategy, but at this point it is clear that their "Consumer as Keeper" model is a wide open invitation to crime. [48]

As the century comes to a close, the opposing "Check Image" model continues to have its own set of problems. Early on in the development of image concepts, many believed that the future lay in image capture and in full transmission of images as the replacement for the truncated paper item. Given the early success that some institutions have had with image statements, this belief was not surprising. Currently reserve banks are deeply involved in working with IBM, Unisys, the U.S. Treasury, and others to develop proposals for image interchange standards in the banking environment. The Federal Reserve is also looking at all aspects of central site archiving and retrieval.

48 "Consumer as Keeper" describes a NACHA check conversion program in which a check is used only for the purpose of scanning the MICR number for later collection via the ACH. The check need not be filled in, however, the check must be returned to the consumer at the point-of-sale. Given the low cost software available to produce perfect MICR checks using such products as VersaCheck, and the ease by which good MICR numbers can be secured, "Consumer as Keeper" is a license to steal. After making all the checks that a thief wants, the robber can enter stores, buy goods, and have the evidence of the crime handed back to them. Short of bank robbery in which all tellers, guards, and other customers instantly forget the face of the thief and the guard hands the thief the video surveillance tape on the way out, I can not imagine a more criminal friendly program.

Check imaging will not reduce the number of checks written by consumers and businesses, but it is likely to lead to a significant reduction in the handling cost of the current paper-based system. Image at the point-of-sale or a kind of "beam the check over" system can keep check clearing intact while taking transportation cost out, but such a system is far from perfected.

The check continues to have a lot of appeal as the twentieth century comes to a close. It continues to be our nation's most familiar payment method, and it works well. We have time-tested standards to support the continued use of the check. We have a national infrastructure for check collection, including the U.S. mail, the check processing capabilities at every depository institution or its agent, local clearings, and correspondent banks.

Most merchants accept checks because consumers use them, and merchants can collect them with relative ease. For electronic payments to supersede check payments, as a nation we will need an array of electronic choices that collectively give consumers and businesses the combination of attributes that they enjoy with checks today; that is, simplicity, universal acceptance, convenience, control, and above all else—low cost. While various media sources continue to suggest that the demise of the check is imminent, the truth is that "little work has been done to examine consumer choice of monetary vehicles and their reaction to changes in the costs associated with value transfer".[49] With a gross loss of just over 1% the check remains the nation's least expensive payment alternative.

The best summary of the state of the paper check as we near the twenty-first century comes from Dr. Alan Lipis' speech entitled ***In Homage to the King: Long Live the Check:*** "It will not be easy to dethrone the

> *"I feel extremely comfortable about going on the record as believing that we will never see a checkless, cashless society in this country. The paper check remains the cheaper, faster, and easier-to-use alternative."*
>
> *Paul Martaus*
> *Martaus & Associates*

49 Anthony M. Santomero and John J. Seater, *Alternative Monies and the Demand for Media of Exchange,* The Wharton School, University of Pennsylvania, May 1996, p. 6.

paper check as the number one choice for bill payers. It is accurate, acceptable, final, private, secure, low-cost, convenient, relatively fast, and a habit for us all."

The best indication of the mindset of banking on the subject of checks comes from Federal Reserve Chairman Alan Greenspan's Rivlin Report, published in January 1998: "Nevertheless, while the checkless society has been predicted for several decades, checks remain the most widely used noncash payment instrument in the United States, representing about three-quarters of all noncash transactions. Despite the development of alternative retail payment methods—credit cards, debit cards, and electronic transfers, such as ACH—the volume of checks has continued to increase over time, albeit at a somewhat slower rate in recent years. Rapid growth in the overall volume of retail payments has allowed for double-digit increases in the volume of electronic retail payments without diminishing check volume."[50]

Banks have good reason to be concerned about the future of the paper check; NACHA is doing everything within its power to move paper to ACH. While this is totally understandable as a competitive move to increase NACHA's market share, a lot is at stake for banks, not the least of which is 16 cents per check in overnight interest, as the last day of float is eliminated in the rush to convert paper to ACH.[51]

50 Committee on the Federal Reserve in the Payments Mechanism, Committee Chair Alice M. Rivlin, January 1998, p. 12.

51 According to a 1996 Federal Reserve Board Study, in 1995, $73.5 trillion worth of checks (including check drawn for securities purchases) were cleared an average of $201 billion per day. The report noted that overnight interest rate for that year averaged about 16 cents per check, or $11.7 billion.

The Evolving Payment System

17

So, the point of this book is that nothing is going to change. No, not quite. The point is that change is slow, and checks have continued to survive many competitive advances.

Think about the very nature of a payment transaction in history. It has always been about trust. Barter as the first payment exchange was based on trust, and as the world moved from barter to valuable minerals, we eventually trusted some sovereign to mint coins to take the place of weighing gold. Of course, in more recent times various payment types and even the payment mechanism itself was gold backed, but as we have moved beyond the gold standard, we have been moving toward virtual transactions.

NBC News recently completed a study of how people feel about the penny. What they found is that really no one, save maybe a coin collector, likes pennies. We won't bend over to pick them up, we wish they could be eliminated from our currency. We think they are worthless. So then, what is next? The nickel? Dimes? Are we detecting a first recognition that there is a direct relationship between the value of a payment mechanism and the effort involved in its use?

Think for a moment about the source of your own vision for what the payment system of the future will look like. If you're anything like me it is probably a cross between Disney's "Tomorrowland," Clark's ***2001*** and Rodenberry's "StarTrek." However, considering the glacier-slow speeds at which the payment system has traditionally evolved, it is hard for most of us to think about any significant change in ten, twenty, or even thirty years. But we can all be assured that change is coming, and the reason is as obvious as why the Internet is sky rocketing and electronic payments are on everyone's minds: physical distances are no longer a barrier to business.

The decline of the check has been over-hyped and anticipated long in advance of any reason. Virtual transactions over the Internet or in physical commerce could well change this pattern, if all forms of payments, not just checks, were to become completely electronic.

So, I start by asking you if you can envision a single method in which cash exchange and credit card settlement could both be preserved in concept, yet eliminated physically. This means that we will not change the basic concept of paying with funds on deposit or that of paying with credit; however, the physicality associated with these payments might well disappear.

Throughout history, the cost of a transaction has had a direct relationship on the success of a business enterprise. Businesses in every industry must always be looking over their shoulder for the new enterprise, which will have significantly lower costs, because that new company can make them obsolete. So it could be with the emergence of cryptographic transactions which carry a digital certificate.

In cash payments today, we already accept two important concepts necessary to the future of non-physical payments. The first is that of the issuance of a ubiquitous and anonymous payment medium called dollars. Why is cash so appealing? It can be exchanged with anyone, it has the lowest cost of exchange, and it is anonymous. In fact, it is one of the primary reasons it exceeds both checks and plastic as a medium of payment. Each payment has a cost of exchange, which declines as we pass a dollar bill from person to person. With an average life of seven months, the cost of this medium is very straightforward: it is the cost to produce or replace a dollar, divided by the average number of times it is used for payment within its useful life. The second concept is the fact that each bill has a digital certificate associated with it. It is called a serial number and is backed by the U.S. government.

So for our purposes, imagine a series of electronic exchanges of value floating between trading partners that have no communications, printing, or creation costs (or at least costs that require several digits to the right of the decimal place). Imagine still that the transaction denomination is but a fraction of a cent, and each has a digital certificate associated with it, backed by the U.S. government as certificate authority. This means that these transactions, in essence, become electronic gold certificates or bearer bonds.[52]

52" What's a Geodesic Economy?" http://www.shipwright.com/rants/rant_22.html.

With this design, all other forms of payment could be eliminated. No need for interchange, as in credit cards today, because the message is the payment, and the payment is the message. Checks become simply authorizations to pay, based on a signature, and are forwarded electronically to a drawee bank. Imagine the check as an encrypted message digitally signed and authenticated, differing from cash only by the fact that the exchange with others is not completed face to face.

While cryptographic transactions that carry a digital certificate are perfectly possible today, some believe that such a direction would bring chaos and anarchy to an otherwise sound payment system. Therefore, a number of people are investigating different approaches to remove the physicality from the payment system. Such approaches include giving a birth certificate to a microprocessor, so that the embedded ID takes the place of the credit or debit card swipe to eliminate card not present as a notion in our card payment system.

A unique microprocessor serial number and strong consumer biometrics interfaces, aligned with a universal payment system interface standard, could allow thousands of devices that are already infrared-ready to communicate, and collectively eliminate the need for consumer plastics or ID. We probably all realize that we live in a time when we no longer need an external device (credit card or otherwise) to identify who we are. Our physical person can do this just fine—but then again, we may be on the brink of an even more basic change in concept.

Today's financial payments system relies on what would be considered insecure book entries. However, these book entries are moved around on very secure networks (NASDAQ Level 3, NIDS, SWIFT, ACH systems, and, of course, MasterCard and Visa networks, for example) which have stringent access controls and strong biometrics identity.

To put this in what I hope is clearer terms, the process for bankcard payments we identify as the "electronic bankcard settlement" continues to be a book-entry system that is really not very high-tech. While paper is no longer the originator of settlement, the electronic entry must yet have a book entry on the part of a number of intermediaries, to conclude payment. A real solution to all of this really is Digital Bearer Certificates.

In the middle 1980s, a cryptographer named David Chaum invented a cryptographic financial protocol, called blind digital signatures, that enables the creation of digital bearer certificates. These certificates could be passed around on the Internet or in physical commerce, just like those physical intaglio certificates of the past.

As an example, I can hand you a digital bearer certificate, which you can inspect online in realtime to see if it's genuine. You can take that certificate (which, in the process of validating, is now actually a reissued certificate which only you can spend) and hand it to someone else in exchange for something valuable. That person can hand that to someone else, and so forth, until the final person in the chain goes back to the issuer and redeems it. (This is all, of course, with the understanding that with this payment direction, no other form of payment is really ever necessary again. Meaning it isn't necessary to ever exchange it for anything physical.)

We can today use David Chaum's cryptographic protocol, which I believe we will look back in the mid twenty-first century and view as an event as important as the invention of the light bulb, the phone, or even the computer, to create bearer forms of practically anything financial: digital bearer bonds, stocks, futures, options, foreign exchange settlement, even personal bearer notes instead of credit card charges. Some financial cryptographers joke about gold-pressed latium futures (for the Star-Trek fans), which gives a hint to just how powerful these cryptographic blobs of ones and zeroes could someday be as abstractors of value.

Now you may or may not agree with either my "beam me over some money" idea or the fact that all of the technology necessary to make this concept happen is already here...now, but then that must be because you missed the following press release in July 1999 about the start-up venture known as

Confinity (Con-Fin-ity: The name conjures-up thoughts of confidentiality and infinity of exchange, both which I believe will be necessary for tomorrow's payment system.)

> ***On July 25, a venture capitalist beamed his $3 million investment through his Palm organizer to the happy CEO sitting across the coffee-shop table. Patrons munching their poached eggs and hash browns couldn't actually see the flurry of money flying through the air, but that's virtually (pardon the pun) what happened. Within seconds, the words: "Would you like to accept the money?" popped up on Con-fin-ity C.E.O. Peter A. Thiel's Palm organizer, which became the official launch of PayPal, an instant service that allows people to exchange money between one another, through their Palm organizers.***

So is tomorrow's payment system here today? Do we all have to start our learning curve all over again, just when we were getting good at the payment system we already know? The answer is, of course, that changes will take time, but we should assume that the virtual world is going to invade our physical world more quickly than most of us imagine, and the check, perhaps in virtual form, may even survive this change.

Data Review

18

In the past few years, we have seen a slow, yet almost imperceptible decline in the growth rate of checks, from 2.7% in 1994 to 2.0% in 1998. We anticipate the growth level to fall just below 1% between 2002 and 2004. With that said, the number of new checks being added to the system each year is still quite impressive with 1.4 billion new checks coming into the system in 2000 and another three-quarters of a billion items or more each year through 2005.

These numbers are very conservative estimates compared to purer linear regression analysis using the last five years of data. Using a double Exponential Smoothing regression model the 2005 data forecasts 5.8% higher transactions levels than our prediction, or 4.3 billion more items. (Note: The lowest model forecasts at 1.8% less than my predication in 2005. Something between minimum growth and medium growth is most likely the correct forecast.)

This forecast continues to mark the conservatism in my forecasting at about the same level that I understated the Federal Reserve processing for 1996. The dollar value of my predictions is even more conservative than my transaction predictions, compared to the purer linear regression analysis. That model forecasts a dollar value 30.6% greater than my predictions principally due to the fact that the average ticket grew so much in the last five years. My prediction assumes a 2.8% increase in average ticket growth through 2005, even though the actual ticket growth during the last five years has been 12.4%.

Federal Reserve Information

(25% of U.S. Check Clearing)

The Federal Reserve Bank system publishes an annual ***Report of Operations in Principal Departments of Federal Reserve Banks***. This annual report compiles information about checks handled by the Federal Reserve banks both in terms of the numbers of checks and in terms of their dollar value.

For three years (1993 to 1995) check processing volume by the Federal Reserve banks declined (dropped nearly 13% in just one year, from 1993 to 1994), during the same period check processing volume in the private sector increased.

According to the Federal Reserve, "Clearing house volume picked up in 1994, largely at the expense of Federal Reserve-cleared volume, due to market adjustments related to the implementation of the same-day settlement amendments to the Federal Reserve Board's Regulation CC. This trend appears to have continued, though to a lesser degree, through the first half of 1995."[53]

53 National Organization of Clearing Houses and the National Automated Clearing House Association, op. cit., *Check Collection Environment*, p. 22.

The National Clearing House Association (NCHA) reporting on NCHA as an alternative clearing mechanism states, "...NCHA today provides a private clearing house alternative in every Federal Reserve Bank district. It clears more than 3 million checks a day, worth some $2.2 billion, and its clearing volumes are expanding more than 10% monthly."[54]

54 Buddy Massengill, NCHA President and Ned Miltko, NCHA Administration, "NCHA Private Check-Clearing Alternative," *Bank Management*, March/April, 1995.

The few years that Federal Reserve transactions and volume were declining while the private clearing mechanism was growing turned out to be less a trend than an event. In fact, the process began to reverse itself as the decade wore on. This short-term decline in Federal Reserve transactions, in particular, a 12.9% decline in transactions and a 13.8% decline in dollar volume for 1994, was incorrectly interpreted by some as an indication of a decline in checks generally, rather than as simply a movement between clearing mechanisms, which will be addressed further in the tables and analysis that follows.

Checks at the Federal Reserve grew 4.3% in dollar volume and 2.4% in transactions in 1997.

Two important elements are noteworthy in the analysis of the Federal Reserve data. The first is that although the annual report from the Board of Governors of the Federal Reserve is the source of the data I have used for Federal Reserve check clearing since 1985, I have subsequently found the 1997 published data to be less than complete. I have received the 1995 through 1998 Planning and Control System (PACS) expense report from Federal Reserve Bank Operations, which in turn is the source for the raw data for each year's Federal Reserve annual report.

This PACS report is used to measure the cost and efficiencies of the Fed, and has the source transaction volume and dollar value of the checks processed by the Fed as well as the average personnel number, unit costs, number of financial institution end points, and the number of transaction items passed through the Federal Reserve System.

The raw data on commercial checks for 1996 in the PACS report is essentially the same as that in the final Annual Report. PACS reported the 1996 commercial check volume which passing through the Federal Reserve as 15,477 million items, while the annual report set the number at 15,487 million commercial check items, plus U.S. government checks and postal money orders. I have not used the PACS data for 1996 or 1997 in Table 5, because I believe that there has been a change in reporting methods, and I suspect that this may not be a good "apples to apples" comparison. The 1997 PACS data reflects 16,093 million items, while the Annual Report reflects 15,949 million items. This difference is 0.9% and renders a 3.0% increase overall in transactions for 1997 (3.9% without government checks), an increase which would otherwise have been 3.4% in transactions.

The second important item to note is that, while the Federal Reserve reported, "The Reserve banks handled 15.5 billion checks in 1996 (excluding U.S. Government checks and postal money orders), about the same number as in 1995,"[55] checks grew to 15.9 billion items in 1997. Although I had anticipated that checks at the Federal Reserve would decline 1% each year through the end of the decade, checks actually grew 2.4% in transactions. Check value also grew 4.3% in 1997 because the average check grew 2% as well.[56]

Both the number and dollar value of checks handled by the Federal Reserve proved to be greater than I projected in 1997. All checks increased, exceeding my forecast by 6.6% in check transactions and 8.1% in the value of checks cleared through

55 Board of Governors of the Federal Reserve System, *Annual Report,* (Washington, DC: published report, 1996), p. 259.

56 Annual detailed report by Federal Reserve Office, PACS Expense Report, Internal Report of the Federal Reserve Bank System, Service Line: Financial Institution & the Public-3000, Service: Commercial Checks- 3360, Activity: Commercial Check Processing-3362, 1997, p. 253. Also 1996, p. 244.

CHICAGO, June 30, 1998

Leaders from the banking and technology industries today announced that the U.S. Government made its first payment over the Internet. The historic transaction is the result of a collaborative three-year research initiative to use the Internet to make check processing more efficient.

The U.S. Treasury's Financial Management Service (FMS) issued the first eCheck payment to GTE Internetworking in payment of a government contract. The payment was made from the Defense Finance and Accounting Service (DFAS), Columbus Center.

the Federal Reserve for 1997. A small contributor to this difference in my previous forecast is the fact that the mandated elimination of government checks by 1999 progressed much slower than earlier anticipated.

As we know, the January 1, 1999 deadline of the federal mandate to eliminate checks written by the federal government was missed—in part because of consumer resistance, but more importantly because of inadequacies in the system the planners counted on to replace checks.

The ACH system, on which the transition from paper checks to electronic payment relied, is as yet incapable of handling the volume and complexity of the federal payment load. In order for the government to use the ACH process effectively, between 6,000 and 7,000 institutions that handle commercial payments need to be able to accept and pass on to customers electronic formatted remittance details. According to the National Automated Clearing House Association (NACHA), only about 1,250 depository institutions nationwide are capable of both receiving and transmitting remittance information with ACH payments.

What should be noted for tracking the Federal Reserve's check item clearing activity in the future is that the government's Financial Management Services (FMS) has been considering eChecks (see box at left) as a way of meeting the goal of eliminating physical check payments. According to the Treasury, eChecks will work like physical checks, retaining float, ubiquity, and universality, but will appear as an electronic image, not as a piece of paper. Because these items will still be handled through the existing check clearing system, albeit loaded as a database rather than through a check sorter, eCheck transactions will still be cleared by the Federal Reserve, and may well appear as check items still clearing through the system.[57]

57 *Bank Technology News*, November 1997, p. 38.

From 1993 to 1995 Federal Reserve check transactions and volume were declining, while the Private Clearing mechanism was growing. This trend of check movement from the Federal Reserve to private clearing is not reflected during 1996 or 1997, and one can actually see some movement to reverse this previous direction. While differences between private and Federal Reserve pricing existed as a motivator to the earlier movement toward the private sector, and Reg. CC's same-day settlement amendment certainly made banks look for longer processing windows and faster availability of funds, the movement was also driven by the concern that the Federal Reserve might not stay in check processing (it's single biggest job since its inception in 1913). However, in early 1998, the Rivlin Report reaffirmed the Federal Reserves' intention to continue as a viable source for check clearing, since the Rivlin committee found that it was important for the Federal Reserve to be in this business segment, as it is likely that the evolving payment mechanism will still include checks for some time to come.

Pulling all the Federal Reserve data together for 1997, we learn that the reserve banks handled 16.5 billion checks, an increase of 2.5% over 1996. The volume of fine-sort check deposits, which are presorted by the depositing bank according to paying bank, increased 0.7% in 1997, compared with an 11.9% decline in 1996. The volume of checks deposited that required processing by reserve banks rose 3.4%.

To increase the efficiency of the check-collection system, the reserve banks continued to expand the use of electronics in check processing. During 1997, the reserve banks electronically presented approximately 2.2 billion checks, or 14.1% of all checks presented to paying banks, an increase of about 56% over the 1996 level. Both the number of checks presented electronically and the number of checks truncated grew in 1997. While electronics or truncation may have been expected to reduce the number of checks, in fact, the increase in checks was quite significant. It is also worthy of note that check growth was neutral from 1995 to 1996, and grew 2.5% from 1996 to 1997. During this same period ACH grew 15.9% from 1995 to 1996 and only 9.7% from 1996 to 1997.

It should be further noted that the number and dollar value of the U.S. government checks or postal money orders handled by the Federal Reserve represents only 4% of both the number and dollar value processed in 1995. In addition, the average check size is observed to be $749 with government checks and money orders, and $748 without government checks or money orders for 1995, rising to $761 by 1999.

Table 4 (see next page) reports the actual number and value of checks handled by the Federal Reserve banks from 1985 to 1997, as well as a subset of these checks titled "No Gov't" which ***excludes*** U.S. Government checks and postal money orders,[58] and extends this check history thorough the year 2005, based on the growth and decline trends over the last three years, plus the elimination of government checks by 2002. (The actual calculation over the last three years is a decline of 93 basis points, with the last two known years being neutral or increasing, respectively.)

Nowhere was the failure of the government's "check elimination mandate" (EFT '99), intended to eliminate check writing by the government by January 1, 1999, more obvious than in the area of benefits payments. Check transactions declined very little from 1998 to 1999 in spite of a nationwide campaign to shift social security and SSI payments to direct deposit.[59] Although the number of benefits payments overall declined .2% from the fourth quarter 1998 to the first quarter 1999, checks remained 28% of all benefits payments, declining less than 100K transactions per quarter. The government's greatest success in check elimination was in the vendor payment area, but although vendor payments declined 6.9% (1999 over 1998), checks continued to represent 51% of all vendor payments.

1998 reflects the same confirmation of growth on all clearing fronts, even though some segments within these three clearing segments differ widely in the amount of growth, and some actually declined. Like the regular movement between private and Federal Reserve clearing, regional bank mergers and restructuring caused increases in one clearing segment and declines in others. For example, in 1997 the Atlanta branch processed 767 million checks, 10% more than in 1996. In December 1997, the branch processed a monthly volume of 74 million checks, a record that was broken in March 1998 when it processed over 77 million checks. The volume of checks processed during the first quarter of 1998 was higher than dur-

58 Board of Governors of the Federal Reserve System, table 9 "Operations in Principal Departments of Federal Reserve Banks," *Annual Report* (1988), p. 223, (1992), p. 279, (1994), p. 319, (1995), p. 303, (1996), p.303, and (1997), p. 295. According to the 1994 *Annual Report of Federal Banks*, data for years proceeding 1991 do not include items sent to the Reserve Banks by the New York Automated Clearing House.

59 *Federal Government Payments Reporting*, 1st Quarter FY 1999 Payment Volume, http://www.fms.treas.gov/eft/agency/v123198.html, and the 2nd Quarter FY 1999 payment Volume, http://www.fms.treas.gov/eft.agency/v33199.html.

Table 4
Federal Reserve Transactions and Dollar Volume
1985-2005

Dollar Volume and Transactions are Expressed in Millions

	Transactions				Dollars		
Year	Total # of Checks	# of Checks No Gov't	Total Value	$ Value No Gov't	Avg. Check No Gov't	Trans. Growth	Dollar Growth
1985	16,687	15,965	$ 10,105,500	$9,557,753	$605.59		
1986	16,951	16,226	$ 11,164,032	$ 10,546,900	$658.61	1.6%	10.5%
1987	17,720	17,006	$ 12,076,347	$11,453,158	$681.51	4.5%	8.2%
1988	18,314	17,623	$ 12,411,283	$11,789,787	$677.69	3.4%	2.8%
1989	18,702	18,014	$ 12,970,924	$12,321,576	$693.56	2.1%	4.5%
1990	19,304	18,595	$ 13,153,694	$12,514,201	$681.40	3.2%	1.4%
1991	19,412	18,743	$ 12,791,997	$12,164,175	$658.97	0.6%	-2.7%
1992	19,727	19,053	$ 13,850,284	$13,241,785	$702.10	1.6%	8.3%
1993	19,681	19,009	$ 14,622,961	$14,066,518	$743.00	-0.2%	5.6%
1994	17,149	16,479	$ 12,607,350	$12,079,107	$735.17	-12.9%	-13.8%
1995	16,128	15,465	$ 12,082,954	$11,567,820	$749.19	-6.0%	-4.2%
1996	16,129	15,487	$ 12,072,754	$11,584,276	$748.51	0.0%	-0.1%
1997	16,531	15,949	$ 12,597,540	$12,169,087	$762.06	2.5%	4.3%
1998	16,882	16,300	$12,865,260	$12,436,807	$762.08	2.1%	2.1%
1999	17,158	16,626	$13,063,996	$12,685,543	$761.40	1.6%	1.5%
2000	17,357	16,875	$13,204,279	$12,875,826	$760.74	1.2%	1.1%
2001	17,307	16,875	$13,154,279	$12,875,826	$760.04	-0.3%	-0.4%
2002	17,085	16,707	$12,975,521	$12,747,068	$759.49	-1.3%	-1.4%
2003	16,917	16,539	$12,646,061	$12,619,597	$747.52	-1.0%	-2.5%
2004	16,752	16,374	$12,519,865	$12,493,401	$747.36	-1.0%	-1.0%
2005	16,588	16,210	$12,394,931	$12,368,467	$747.21	-1.0%	-1.0%

Assumptions :The elimination of government checks by the year 2002 and an overall decline in the number and value of checks beginning in 2001.

ing the same period in 1997. In addition, the inter-territory group sort products (checks payable at out-of-zone banks) brought to the Atlanta branch added 7.5 million items in 1997 and 20 million items in 1998.

Private Clearing Information

(42% of U.S. Check Clearing)

Sample data for private clearing has been configured in different ways through the years, based on available data and the composition of the National Organization of Clearing Houses (NOCH) since 1994. NOCH has been the participating organization providing data on which to test overall private clearing volume and transactions, and upon which an average ticket for the on-us check value has been based.

Through the years the composition of data available from private clearing houses has changed. In fact, the data made available to me is from private clearing houses that are board member organizations of the National Organization of Clearing Houses (NOCH). For 1994 through 1997 I received the transactions and dollar value of checks handled by National Clearing House Association (NCHA) and for 1994 and 1995 I received the transactions and dollar value of checks handled by the Kansas City Clearing House. After 1997 and 1995, respectively, these clearing houses were no longer board member banks of NOCH.

Since 1994 the three clearing houses which have been consistent board members and reporting organizations of NOCH have been the New York Clearing House, the California Clearing House, and the Chicago Clearing House. These three organizations have represented at least 8.5% of the national clearing house volume and between 14 and 20% of the dollar value of all checks cleared through private clearing houses in the U.S. each year.

Mid-sized clearing houses including Pittsburgh, Boston, Philadelphia, and Tulsa are excluded from all the tables, including only board member data, and in the later charts NCHA and Southwest Clearing House have been excluded. The 50% decline in value and the 43 million-transaction decline in volume of checks from the New York Clearing House was the result of the discontinuance of checks as a means of settlement of securities transactions. This volume was replaced by wire or ACH settlement beginning at the second quarter of 1996.

New York Clearing House
Transactions and Dollars in Millions

	of Checks	Value of Check	Avg .Check
1994	355	$3,937,909	$11,093
1995	321	$4,046,459	$12,606
1996	278	$2,022,278	$7,274
1997	276	$2,475,092	$8,968
Est. 1998	301	$2,781,133	$9,240

While the New York, California, and Chicago tables provide the information for each of the individual years, Table 5 reflects information from selected board members of the National Organization of Clearing Houses (NOCH) for 1997 and 1998, and provides a representative sample of private clearing trends for the first half of 1998.[60] You will note that that I have forecasted the full year 1998 clearing house numbers for New York, California and Chicago, even though Table 5 has only the first half data for 1997 and 1998. NOCH was unable to provide full year data for 1998 by press time, and I have therefore utilized the first half data for 1997 and 1998 to try and determine current trends, and the full year 1994, 1995, 1996, and 1997 data previously researched. For the previous four years I have pro-

60 National Organization of Clearing Houses, Check Volume, (Herndon, VA: unpublished report, 1998). Data is from the first half of 1997 and 1998 and reflects the information from selected board members of the National Organization of Clearing Houses.

California Clearing House
Transactions and Dollars in Millions

	# of Checks	Value of Check	Avg. Check
1994	1,384	$669,225	$484
1995	1,545	$4703,080	$455
1996	1,544	$755,427	$489
1997	1,425	$677,181	$475
Est. 1998	1,350	$724,300	$537

vided full year information from all board members of NOCH, reflected in Tables 6, 7, and 8—none of which were previously published by NOCH.

No 1998 data was available for National Clearing House Association (NCHA) or the Southwest Clearing House for 1998, although both had increases in dollar and processing volume for 1997.

Chicago Clearing House
Transactions and Dollars in Millions

	# of Checks	Value of Check	Avg. Check
1994	541	$524,608	$970
1995	563	$527,309	$937
1996	590	$554,491	$940
1997	651	$634,995	$975
Est. 1998	696	$713,276	$1,025

For the first half of 1998 compared to the first half of 1997 (see table page 117), the American Clearing House segment grew a whopping 22.7% in dollars and 5.3% in transactions, the California Clearing House increased 6.9% in dollars and declined 5.3% in transactions, and the Chicago Clearing House grew 12.3% in dollars and 6.9% in transactions. In addition to the New York Clearing House's continued rebound from their decline of 1996, 1998 represents growth of 15.0% in dollars and 9.0% in transactions.

Chase also grew 6.3% in dollars and 2.5% in transactions, which, from a total transaction point of view (621 million), was about the same transaction size as American, Chicago, and New York Clearing Houses combined (662 million), which also grew a combined 6.9% in transactions. Based on these five reporting segments, private clearing house growth was 12.4% in dollars and 1% in transactions for the first half of 1998, exclusive of NCHA and Southwest Clearing House which both contributed significantly to the 1997 transaction growth, at 2.4% and 17.9%

Table 5
NOCH Transactions and Dollar Volume
Dollar Value and Transaction Counts are Expressed in Millions

Reporting Clearing House	1997 $	1997 #	1997 Average Check	1998 $	1998 #	1998 Average Check
American (ACHA)	$62,600	170	$367.80	$76,800	179	$428.33
California (BCH)	$336,300	725	$464.18	$359,700	687	$523.58
Chicago (CCHA)	$312,300	317	$984.24	$350,800	339	$1,034.20
Chase	$272,500	606	$449.60	$289,800	621	$466.74
New York (NYCH)	$1,087,500	132	$8,232.40	$1,250,200	144	$8,712.20
Total	$2,071,200	1,950	$1,062.04	$2,327,300	1,970	$1,181.43
Total Less NY	$983,700	$1,818	$541.06	$1,077,100	$1,826	$589.74

Small and mid-sized clearing houses such as Pittsburgh, Boston, Philadelphia, and Tulsa, as well as the National Clearing House Association and the Southwest Clearing House are excluded from the table above.

in transactions, respectively. Our prior year, private clearing house data places the 1995 to 1996 transaction growth at 7.3% and the 1996 to 1997 transaction growth at 3.3%.

Table 6 (see page 119) also reflects information from each board member of the National Organization of Clearing Houses—in this case, full data for 1996 and 1997—and is a representative sample of private clearing trends for 1997. Data for the calendar year 1997 showed a 3.3% increase in transactions and a 12.1% increase in the dollar value of checks handled by the board member banks of NOCH. Concurrently, checks cleared through the Federal Reserve System grew 2.5% in transactions and 4.3% in dollar volume.

As an example, the American Clearing House segment grew 6% in dollars and 1.8% in transactions, the California Clearing House declined 10.4% in dollars and 7.8% in transactions, and the Chicago Clearing House grew a whopping 14.5% in dollars and 10.3% in transactions. The New York Clearing House began a rebound from the decline of 1996 and grew 22.3% in dollars and declined 1% in transactions.

The Southwest Clearing House grew 16.6% in dollars and 17.9% in transactions.[61]

As another subset of the NOCH data, the National Clearing House Association (NCHA) grew from 963 million transactions to 986 million transactions, or 2.4%. In addition to reflecting continued growth in private sector dollar volume, the NOCH information establishes an average ticket for this representative sample of $1,059 with federal clearing house items and $548 without federal items for 1997.

For 1996, Table 7 (see page 121) reflects information from each board member of the National Organization of Clearing Houses, in this case, for 1995 and 1996. The most significant change in data for 1996 is that slightly over half of the dollar volume for New York was eliminated between 1995 and 1996, with a 13.4% decline in transactions for the New York segment. While I had predicated in the 1995 that I expected securities

61 National Organization of Clearing Houses, *Check Volume*, (Herndon, VA: unpublished report, 1998). Data is from 1996 and 1997 and reflects the information from each of the board members of the National Organization of Clearing Houses.

Table 6
NOCH Transactions and Dollar Volume
Dollar Value and Transaction Counts are Expressed in Millions

Geographic Area	1996 Dollars	1996 No.	1996 Average Check	1997 Dollars	1997 No.	1997 Average Check
American	$119,620	333	$359.22	$126,797	339	$374.03
California	$755,427	1,544	$489.27	$677,181	1,425	$475.21
Chicago	$554,491	590	$939.82	$634,995	651	$975.41
Fed. items included in above data	$44,414	48	$925.29	$44,819	47	$953.60
NCHA	$699,652	963	$726.53	$717,990	986	$728.18
New York	$2,022,278	278	$7,274.38	$2,475,092	276	$8,967.72
Southwest	$471,323	1,030	$457.60	$549,532	1,215	$452.29
Fed. items included in above data	$87,910	$124	$708.95	$101,779	$128	$795.15
Total Excluding N.Y/NCHA	$1,900,861	3497	$543.57	$1,988,505	3,630	$547.80
Total	$4,622,791	4,738	$975.68	$5,181,587	4,892	$1,059.20
Fed. items included in above total	$132,324	$172	$769.33	$146,598	$176	$832.94
Net	$4,490,467	4,566	$983.46	$5,034,989	4,716	$1067.64

Small and mid-sized Clearing Houses such as Pittsburgh, Boston, Philadelphia, and Tulsa are excluded from the table above.

transactions in 1996 would be handled in the future by FedWire or ACH, rather than by check, I did not expect all such activity to conclude in the first quarter of 1996.

This historically anomalous element of the private clearing data was resolved at the beginning of the second quarter of 1996 with the 1996 NOCH numbers reflecting a sharp drop in the New York Segment due to securities transactions moving to wire or ACH settlement (T-3). In addition, private clearing numbers also declined due to in-market mergers, such as the Chase and Chemical bank merger, reducing the number of New York NOCH banks from eleven (11) at the beginning of 1995 to only eight (8) at the end of 1996.

This decline, like the 1994 decline in Federal Reserve clearing, was quickly reported in business circles as a general decline in consumer check use, which it was certainly not. In fact, other than the payment method change for checks drawn for securities in the New York segment, growth is reflected overall at NOCH. For example, the American Clearing House segment grew 10.2% in dollars and 2.8% in transactions; the California clearing house grew 7.4% in dollars with virtually no change in transactions; the Chicago Clearing House grew 5.1% in dollars (even though the Fed's clearing dollars in Chicago declined more than 30%) and 4.8% in transactions. The largest growth came from the Southwest clearing house, which grew 19.5% in dollars and 19.1% in transactions.[62]

Table 8 (see page 122) also reflects information from each board member of the National Organization of Clearing Houses, in this case, for 1994 and 1995. This sample grew 12.3% in dollars and 22.2% in transactions when Federal Reserve items cleared through NOCH board member Clearing Houses are included, and increased 11.7% in dollars and 20.0% in transactions when federal clearing house items are excluded, reflecting the decline in federal items and corresponding growth in private sector clearing discussed above.[63]

62 National Organization of Clearing Houses, *Check Volume*, (Herndon, VA: unpublished report, 1997). Data is from 1995 and 1996 and reflects the information from each of the board members of the National Organization of Clearing Houses. Data for Kansas City which was included in the 1996 *Check Growth Study* has been removed from the 1997 report, as Kansas City is no longer a NOCH Board member, and no longer reports data to NOCH. The New York average check is higher than the other segments due to the volume of wholesale checks and securities settlement transactions, early in 1996. Securities transactions began being settled by FedWire or ACH, rather than check at the end of the first quarter of 1996.

63 National Organization of Clearing Houses, *Check Volume*, (Herndon, VA: unpublished report, 1996). Data is from 1994 and 1995 and reflects the information from each of the board members of the National Organization of Clearing Houses. The New York average check is higher than the other segments due to the volume of wholesale checks and securities settlement transactions. The securities transactions are expected to be handled by FedWire or ACH, rather than check, in the future.

Table 7
NOCH Transactions and Dollar Volume
Dollar Value and Transaction Counts are Expressed in Millions

	1995			1996		
Geographic Area	**Dollars**	**No.**	**Average Check**	**Dollars**	**No.**	**Average Check**
American	$108,581	324	$335.13	$119,620	333	$359.22
California	$703,080	1,545	$455.07	$755,427	1,544	$489.27
Chicago	$527,309	563	$936.61	$554,491	590	$939.82
Fed. items included in above data	$64,258	50	$1,285.16	$44,414	48	$925.29
NCHA	$793,877	796	$997.33	$699,652	963	$726.53
New York	$4,046,459	321	$12,605.79	$2,022,278	278	$7,274.38
Southwest	$394,254	865	$455.78	$471,323	1030	$457.60
Fed. items included in above data	$73,846	117	$631.16	$87,910	124	$708.95
Total Excluding N.Y/NCHA	$1,733,224	3297	$525.70	$1,900,861	3,497	$543.57
Total	$6,573,560	4,414	$1,489.25	$4,622,791	4738	$975.68
Fed. items included in above total	$138,104	167	$826.97	$132,324	172	$769.33
Net	$6,435,456	4,247	$1,515.29	$4,490,467	4,566	$983.46

Kansas City Clearing House was no longer a NOCH board member in 1996, and has been excluded from the 1995 data since 1996 data was unavailable. In addition, small and mid-sized clearing houses such as Pittsburgh, Boston, Philadelphia, and Tulsa are excluded from the table above.

Table 8
NOCH Transactions and Dollar Volume
Dollar Value and Transaction Counts are Expressed in Millions

Geographic Area	1994 Dollars	1994 No.	1994 Average Check	1995 Dollars	1995 No.	1995 Average Check
American	$106,872	310	$344.75	$108,581	324	$335.13
California	$669,225	1,384	$483.54	$703,080	1,545	$455.07
Chicago	$524,608	541	$969.70	$527,309	563	$936.61
Fed. items included in above data	$84,340	58	$1,454.54	$64,258	50	$1,285.16
Kansas City	$124,604	193	$645.62	$121,493	186	$653.19
Fed CH Items	$35,658	48	$742.88	$28,775	43	$669.19
NCHA**	$324,955	339	$958.57	$793,877	796	$997.33
New York	$3,937,909	355	$11,092.70	$4,046,459	321	$12,605.79
Southwest	$273,979	641	$427.42	$394,254	865	$455.78
Fed. items included in above data	$0	0	$0	$73,846	117	$631.16
Total Excluding N.Y/NCHA	$1,699,288	3069	$553.69	$1,854,717	3,497	$530.37
Total	$5,962,152	3,763	$1,584.41	$6,695,053	4,600	$1,455.45
Fed. items included in above total	$119,998	106	$1,132.06	$166,879	210	$794.66
Net	$5,842,154	3,657	$1,597.53	$6,528,174	4,390	$1,487.06

My research revealed that the average check size for private clearing in 1998 was $1,181, which remained relatively constant over the last four years; however, because the data was a partial year, I have used the full year 1997 average ticket ($1,059) for overall weighting.

In the footnote to the 1991 data from Bank for International Settlements (BIS) the justification for assuming a U.S. average check value of $1,150, which is slightly greater than my 1997 research results ($1,059), is not explained by BIS. This assumption has been utilized in BIS reports for each of the years 1987 through 1994.[64]

Additionally, I have found two more sources reporting a higher U.S. check average. The first is a study prepared for The Banking Research Fund (BRF), which reports that the National Clearing House Association processed 877,000 transactions a day in the third quarter of 1994, for $1 billion per day, or an average check of $1,140.[65] NOCH also reported in 1996 that, "...a check averaged $1,194".[66]

Given all the available sources, each of which must assume an average check size for the 30% to 33% of "On-Us" bank clearing, depending on the year of the calculation, we end up with a range from $1,059 (my research number explained above) to $1,194, based on the 1996 NOCH data.

National Average Check Size

BIS=	**$1,059**
BRF=	**$1,140**
NOCH=	**$1,194**
Our #=	**$1,059**

For the purposes of the private clearing portion of the check forecast in Table 10 (see pages 128 and 129), I have assumed a $1,059 average check, which is a conservative number for the forecasting model (the overall ticket is $830, see table 9.) Although I believe the $1,059 check average is a reasonable assumption, I acknowledge that it may understate the future check volume by as much as 11%.

64 Committee on Payment and Settlement Systems of the central banks of the Group of Ten Countries, Bank for International Settlements, Statistics on Payment Systems in Eleven Developed Countries (Basle, Switzerland: published report, 1992). United States Section C, p. 48, footnote 1: "Includes 56,797 million commercial cheques valued at USD 65.3 trillion; 418 million traveler's cheques valued at USD 22.5 billion; 855 million money orders valued at USD 81.1 billion (including 166 million US postal money orders valued as USD 17.7 billion); and 521 million federal government cheques valued at USD 723 billion. The Federal Reserve processed 18.7 billion cheques valued at USD 12.2 trillion. The average value of a cheque processed through the Federal Reserve was USD 648; the average value of all cheques processed was about USD 1,150. Thus the total value of all commercial cheques is estimated at USD 65.3 trillion (1,150x56,797)."

65 *Committee on Payment and Settlement Systems of the Central banks of the Group of Ten Countries*, United States Section C, table 8, "Payment instruction by selected payment systems: volume of transactions," p. 107, table 12, "Indicator of use of various cashless payment instruments: volume of transactions," table 10, "Transfer instructions handled by securities settlement systems: volume of transactions," Bank for International Settlements, Statistics on Payment Systems in Ten Countries (December, 1995). Source data noted as Federal Reserve.

On-Us (33% of U.S. Check Clearing)

Table 11 reflects checks handled by private clearing houses, directly between banks, and by the Federal Reserve System. Data for the Federal Reserve system is detailed earlier, and is readily available, however, this data represents only a fraction (25%) of all checks written in the United States. Although the National Organization of Clearing Houses compiles various reports, as does the American Bankers Association, only limited data exists on the volume of checks or the dollar value of checks cleared through private clearing efforts or "On-Us" items.

The base data for the information in Table 11 is drawn from the Bank for International Settlements report titled, ***Statistics on Payment Systems in the Group of Ten Countries***. In addition, data was drawn from 1987 and 1989 reports on the relative importance of cashless payment instruments in the payment system. This data provides baseline information for 1990 through 1995 volume of checks processed outside the Federal Reserve System, with 1994 data confirmed by the 1996 ***Report of the Settlement Risk Management Task Force: Findings and Recommendations***.

Summary Level Check Forecast

Tables 5 through 8 provide important information about the overall average check amount. In 1998, the Federal Reserve served as the clearing mechanism for 25% of the checks processed in the United States, with a $762 average check amount. Private clearing mechanisms (clearing house, correspondents, and direct sends) processed 42% of checks, with a $1,059 average check amount, for 1997, and early 1998 data (first half) indicates what may be a $122 increase due entirely to ticket growth at the New York Clearing House.

Given the addition of another 33% of "On-Us" bank clearing as the remaining clearing mechanism, the "On-Us" check average is likely to reflect the average of the National Organization of Clearing Houses, less the New York segment. I have historically taken the New York data out of the "on-us" calculation, to

66 1989 Data: Group of Experts on Payment Systems of the central banks of the group of Ten Countries, *Bank for International Settlements, Statistics on Payment Systems in the Group of Eleven Developed Countries* (Basle, Switzerland, December, 1990), Section C, p. 47. No source data noted. 1987 Data: Prepared under the aegis of the Bank for International Settlements by the Central Banks of the Group of Ten Countries and Switzerland, Payment Systems in Eleven Developed Countries, Third Edition, (Chicago, IL: Bank Administration Institute, published report, 1989), United States, Country Tables, Item C, p. 291. No source data noted.

tone down the effect of this very unusual check average. With a $548 average check amount for 1997 and early 1998 data (first half) reflecting what may be a $42 increase, I was inclined to raise the "On-Us" ticket for 1998 because neither the missing NCHA or Southwest Clearing House data would have driven the 1998 ticket down. The Table 9 calculation (see below) reflects an average check of $590, (the 1998, half year, Table 5 total less New York) and creates an overall weighted average check amount, as follows, of $830:

Table 9
Check Clearing Mechanisms

Mechanism	% of Total	Check Amount
Private Clearing	42%	$1,059
Bank On-Us Clearing	33%	$590
Federal Reserve Clearing	25%	$762
Total	100%	$830

As noted earlier in the private clearing explanation, each year through 1995, the New York average check size had driven the national check average upward significantly because of large checks in the New York segment written for securities purchases. Table 11 (see page 128) reflects the historical data including checks for securities purchases.

This historically anomalous element of the private clearing data was reduced dramatically at the beginning of the second quarter of 1996 with the 1996 NOCH numbers showing a sharp drop in the New York Segment due to securities transactions moving to wire or ACH settlement (T-3). Table 12 (see page 130) reflects the data also shown in Table 10, which has further been extended into 2005.

Tables 11 and 12 will help the reader to see the impact of the change by comparing the total historical check data by check clearing channel, as reported by the Federal Reserve and by Committee on Payment and Settlement Systems of the Central Banks of the Group of Ten countries, before checks drawn for securities settlements were extracted and after such checks are excluded.

67 1987 Data: Prepared under the aegis of the Bank for International Settlements by the Central Banks of the Group of Ten Countries and Switzerland, *Payment Systems in Eleven Developed Countries*, Third Edition, (Chicago, IL: Bank Administration Institute, published report, 1989), United States, Country Tables, Item C, p. 291. No source data noted. 1989 Data: Group of Experts on Payment Systems of the central banks of the group of Ten Countries, Bank for International Settlements, Statistics on Payment Systems in the Group of Eleven Developed Countries (Basle, Switzerland, December, 1990), Section C, p. 47. No source data noted. 1992 through 1997 Data: Committee on Payment and Settlement Systems of the Central Banks of the Group of Ten Countries, Bank for International Settlements, Statistics on Payment Systems in the Group of Ten Countries Basle, Switzerland, December, 1997, and 1998), Table 8, p.99 and 101 through 105. Source data noted for some number, as Federal Reserve and national Automated Clearing House Association.

In comparing the data, it becomes clear that when interpreting various check sources, the reader must know if checks drawn for securities have or have not been extracted from the data. The value of such transactions is very significant, ranging from $9,770.7 billion in 1985 to $15,784.9 billion in 1995.

It is most important to note that while the current research permits the exclusion of the checks drawn for the settlement of securities transactions, which have always masked the actual value of commercial checks and skewed the U.S. check average, the number of checks are unchanged in the forecast and historical numbers. These checks, while representing significant dollars, represented less than one tenth of one percent of the number of checks written each year and are essentially covered in rounding to the nearest million transactions.

Tables

Table 10
Actual[67] and Projected Transactions & Dollar Volume 1985-2005.

Including Fed Clearing, Private Clearing, and the 33% of all checks cleared by the bank on which they are drawn. Excluding checks drawn for Securities Purchases.
Dollar Value and Transaction Counts are Expressed in millions

Transactions

Date	Total U.S. Checks	Private Clearing	On-Us	Federal Reserve
1985	44,720	16,546	11,487	16,687
1986	46,960	17,375	12,634	16,951
1987	49,200	18,204	13,276	17,720
1988	50,990	18,356	14,320	18,314
1989	52,900	19,044	15,154	18,702
1990	55,397	19,944	16,149	19,304
1991	57,465	20,689	17,364	19,412
1992	58,399	21,024	17,648	19,727
1993	60,297	22,527	18,089	19,681
1994	61,670	26,221	18,300	17,149
1995	62,963	28,145	18,690	16,128
1996	64,684	29,852	18,703	16,129
1997	66,093	27,759	21,803	16,531
1998	67,415	28,286	22,247	16,882
1999	68,763	28,913	22,692	17,158
2000	70,138	29,636	23,146	17,357
2001	70,840	30,156	23,377	17,307
2002	71,548	30,852	23,611	17,085
2003	72,264	31,500	23,847	16,917
2004	72,986	32,149	24,085	16,752
2005	73,716	32,802	24,326	16,588

Table 10
Actual[67] and Projected Transactions & Dollar Volume 1985-2005.

Including Fed Clearing, Private Clearing, and the 33% of all checks cleared by the bank on which they are drawn. Excluding checks drawn for Securities Purchases.
Dollar Value and Transaction Counts are Expressed in millions

		Dollars		
Total U.S. Checks	**Private Clearing**	**On-Us**	**Federal Reserve**	**Average Checks**
$32,109,188	$15,892,817	$6,110,871	$10,105,500	$718.01
$34,574,093	$16,688,880	$6,721,182	$11,164,032	$736.25
$36,624,121	$17,484,942	$7,062,832	$12,076,347	$744.39
$37,660,461	$17,630,938	$7,618,240	$12,411,283	$738.59
$39,324,614	$18,291,762	$8,061,928	$12,970,924	$743.38
$40,901,174	$19,156,212	$8,591,268	$13,153,694	$738.33
$41,901,430	$19,871,785	$9,237,648	$12,791,997	$729.16
$43,432,572	$20,193,552	$9,388,736	$13,850,284	$743.72
$45,883,493	$21,637,184	$9,623,348	$14,622,961	$760.96
$47,528,221	$25,185,271	$9,735,600	$12,607,350	$770.69
$49,003,237	$27,033,273	$9,887,010	$12,082,954	$778.29
$51,412,590	$29,165,404	$10,174,432	$12,072,754	$794.83
$54,852,422	$29,396,781	$12,858,101	$12,597,540	$829.93
$56,081,243	$30,096,257	$13,119,889	$12,865,097	$831.88
$57,366,046	$30,908,334	$13,382,287	$13,075,425	$834.26
$58,705,794	$31,828,787	$13,649,933	$13,227,075	$837.00
$59,513,371	$32,537,967	$13,786,432	$13,188,972	$840.11
$60,387,980	$33,443,889	$13,924,296	$13,019,795	$844.02
$61,258,447	$34,303,139	$14,063,539	$12,891,769	$847.71
$62,141,030	$35,170,826	$14,204,175	$12,766,029	$851.41
$63,036,494	$36,049,226	$14,346,216	$12,641,051	$855.12

Table 11
1985 through 1995 Transactions and Volume
Including Checks for Securities Purchases
Dollar Value and Transaction Counts are Expressed in Millions

Date	Transactions Total U.S. Checks	Private Clearing	On-Us	Federal Reserve
1985	44,720	16,546	11,487	16,687
1986	46,960	17,375	12,634	16,951
1987	49,200	18,204	13,276	17,720
1988	50,990	18,356	14,320	18,314
1989	52,900	19,044	15,154	18,702
1990	55,397	19,944	16,149	19,304
1991	57,465	20,689	17,364	19,412
1992	58,399	21,024	17,648	19,727
1993	60,297	22,527	18,089	19,681
1994	61,670	26,221	18,300	17,149
1995	62,963	28,145	18,690	16,128

Table 11
1985 through 1995 Transactions and Volume Including Checks for Securities Purchases
Dollar Value and Transaction Counts are Expressed in Millions

Dollars				
Total U.S. Checks	Private Clearing	On-Us	Federal Reserve	Average Checks
$41,879,838	$25,663,466	$6,110,871	$10,105,500	$936.49
$44,834,149	$26,948,935	$6,721,182	$11,164,032	$954.73
$47,373,583	$28,234,404	$7,062,832	$12,076,347	$962.88
$48,499,679	$28,470,156	$7,618,240	$12,411,283	$951.16
$50,570,096	$29,537,244	$8,061,928	$12,970,924	$955.96
$52,678,106	$30,933,144	$8,591,268	$13,153,694	$950.92
$54,118,284	$32,088,639	$9,237,648	$12,791,997	$941.76
$55,847,244	$32,608,224	$9,388,736	$13,850,284	$956.30
$59,185,686	$34,939,377	$9,623,348	$14,622,961	$981.57
$63,011,721	$40,668,771	$9,735,600	$12,607,350	$1,021.76
$65,622,859	$43,652,895	$9,887,010	$12,082,954	$1,042.24

Table 12

1985 through 1995 Transactions and Volume
Excluding Checks for Securities Purchases

Dollar Value and Transaction Counts are Expressed in Millions

	Transactions			
Date	**Total U.S. Checks**	**Private Clearing**	**On-Us**	**Federal Reserve**
1985	44,720	16,546	11,487	16,687
1986	46,960	17,375	12,634	16,951
1987	49,200	18,204	13,276	17,720
1988	50,990	18,356	14,320	18,314
1989	52,900	19,044	15,154	18,702
1990	55,397	19,944	16,149	19,304
1991	57,465	20,689	17,364	19,412
1992	58,399	21,024	17,648	19,727
1993	60,297	22,527	18,089	19,681
1994	61,670	26,221	18,300	17,149
1995	62,963	28,145	18,690	16,128

Table 12
1985 through 1995 Transactions and Volume Excluding Checks for Securities Purchases
Dollar Value and Transaction Counts are Expressed in Millions

Dollars

Total U.S. Checks	Private Clearing	On-Us	Federal Reserve	Average Checks
$32,109,188	$15,892,817	$6,110,871	$10,105,500	$718.01
$34,574,093	$16,688,880	$6,721,182	$11,164,032	$736.25
$36,624,121	$17,484,942	$7,062,832	$12,076,347	$744.39
$37,660,461	$17,630,938	$7,618,240	$12,411,283	$738.59
$39,324,614	$18,291,762	$8,061,928	$12,970,924	$743.38
$40,901,174	$19,156,212	$8,591,268	$13,153,694	$738.33
$41,901,430	$19,871,785	$9,237,648	$12,791,997	$729.16
$43,432,572	$20,193,552	$9,388,736	$13,850,284	$743.72
$45,883,493	$21,637,184	$9,623,348	$14,622,961	$760.96
$47,528,221	$25,185,271	$9,735,600	$12,607,350	$770.69
$49,003,237	$27,033,273	$9,887,010	$12,082,954	$778.29

Appendix

Transaction Volume Forecast-Most Recent 5 Year Data

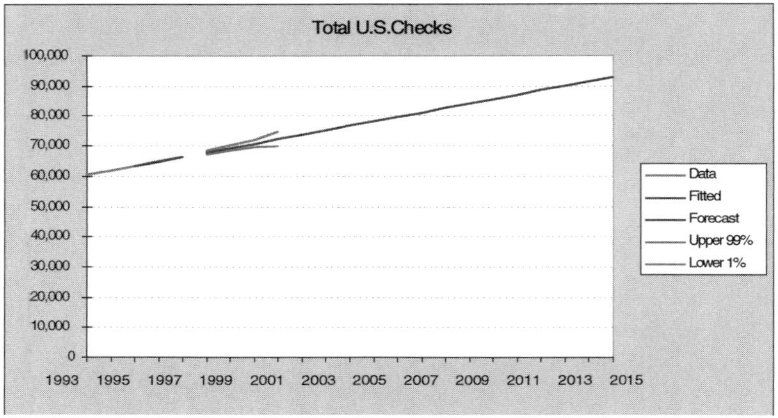

Method Errors:

	Method	**RMSE**	**MAD**	**MAPE**
Best:	Double Exponential Smoothing	214.56	147.64	0.23%
2nd:	Single Moving Average	1458.1	1449	2.27%
3rd:	Single Exponential Smoothing	1459.2	1450.1	2.27%

Method Statistics:

	Method	Durbin-Watson	Theil's U
Best:	Double Exponential Smoothing	2.374	0.165
2nd:	Single Moving Average	0.034	1
3rd:	Single Exponential Smoothing	0.255	1.001

Method Parameters:

	Method	**Parameter**	**Value**
Best:	Double Exponential Smoothing	Alpha	0.791
		Beta	0.5
2nd:	Single Moving Average	Periods	1
3rd:	Single Exponential Smoothing	Alpha	0.999

		Forecast	
Date	**Lower 1%**	**Forecast**	**Upper 99%**
1998	66,954	67,578	68,202
1999	68,231	69,063	69,895
2000	69,300	70,548	71,796
2001	69,537	72,033	74,529
2002		73,517	
2003		75,002	
2004		76,487	
2005		77,972	
2006		79,457	
2007		80,942	
2008		82,427	
2009		83,912	
2010		85,396	
2011		86,881	
2012		88,366	
2013		89,851	
2014		91,336	
2015		92,821	

Summary:

Number of series: 1
Periods to forecast: 18
Seasonality: none
Error Measure: MAD

Series: Total U.S.Checks

Method:Double Exponential Smoothing
Parameters:
Alpha: 0.791
Beta: 0.500
Error: 147.64

Dollar Volume Forecast-Most Recent 5 Year Data

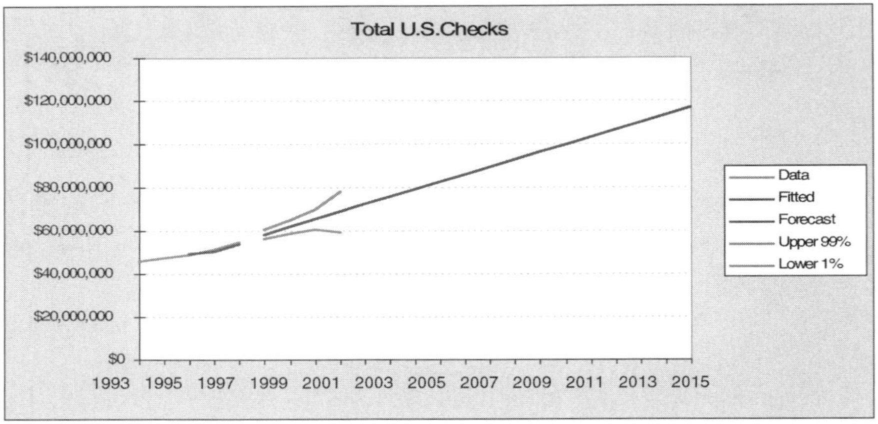

Method Errors:

	Method	RMSE	MAD	MAPE
Best:	Double Exponential Smoothing	810114	712330	1.35%
2nd:	Single Moving Average	2372669	2242232	4.36%
3rd:	Single Exponential Smoothing	2374173	2243615	4.36%

Method Statistics:

	Method	Durbin-Watson	Theil's U
Best:	Double Exponential Smoothing	0.624	0.334
2nd:	Single Moving Average	0.087	1
3rd:	Single Exponential Smoothing	0.207	1.001

Method Parameters:

	Method	Parameter	Value
Best:	Double Exponential Smoothing	Alpha	0.999
		Beta	0.999
2nd:	Single Moving Average	Periods	1
3rd:	Single Exponential Smoothing	Alpha	0.999

Forecasts			
Date	**Lower 1%**	**Forecast**	**Upper 99%**
1998	$55,934,007	$58,290,089	$60,646,171
1999	$58,587,346	$61,728,789	$64,870,232
2000	$60,455,325	$65,167,489	$69,879,654
2001	$59,181,860	$68,606,190	$78,030,519
2002		$72,044,890	
2003		$75,483,590	
2004		$78,922,290	
2005		$82,360,990	
2006		$85,799,690	
2007		$89,238,391	
2008		$92,677,091	
2009		$96,115,791	
2010		$99,554,491	

Summary:

Number of series:	1
Periods to forecast:	18
Seasonality:	none
Error Measure:	MAD

Series: Total U.S.Checks

Method: Double Exponential Smoothing

Parameters:

Alpha:	0.999
Beta:	0.999
Error:	712330

Where Previous Check Study Data Is In Use

Previous check research developed by the author and used in this book has been distributed by a variety of banking and financial institutions including CoreStates Financial Corporation, HSBC group, Marine Midland, National Bank of the Redwoods, Bear Stearns, and the National Organizations of Clearing Houses (NOCH). CoreStates presented the material to 200 university and college bursars at their Bursar, Cashier, and Treasury Management Conferences in 1996 and 1997. HSBC distributed the 1997 material to all senior vice presidents worldwide in May 1998 and to Community Bankers Merchant Services in 1999. In addition, Standard Federal Bank presented the check material at a Fraud and Forgery presentation for members of the Institute of Financial Education, as well as the Bank Security Officers Association, in 1997 and 1998.

The 1998 check data was presented by the author at The Check Forum sponsored by Global Concepts in May 1998. Participating banks included Chase Manhattan Bank, Fleet Financial Group, Regions Financial Corporation, Wachovia, First Commercial Corporation, Barclays Bank, BankBoston, BankOne, and NationsBank, to name but a few. The check data was also presented to all participants at Chexpo '98 including the Vice Chair of the Federal Reserve.

The 1999 check data has been presented by the author to the Check Payments Systems Association (CPSA), and was a core source of data for ***The Indelible Check: An Assessment of the Dominance of the Check in the United States Payment System at the Close of the 20th Century***, published by Global Concepts on behalf of the CPSA.

Portions of author's check data are used daily in the specialized marketing materials of a variety of entities, including the nationally recognized magazine ***Collection & Credit Risk***, December 1996; ***Business Today***, printed for the Canadian market October 26, 1997; ***Item Processing Report*** (Phillips Publishing), October 1997; ***American Demographics***, March 1998; The Southland Corporation, continuously since February 1998; ***Marketing Tools***, April 1998; ***San Jose Mercury-News***,

June 8, 1998; ***Saint Paul Pioneer Press***, June 18, 1998; the promotional materials of VeriFone, a Hewlett-Packard Company, in its "The U.S. Check Market" white paper since September 1998; ImageSoft Technologies' newsletter, ***Image Inquiry***, beginning September 1998; ***Chain Store Age***, October 1998; IVI CheckMate in its "Electronic Check Conversion" white paper, beginning mid 1998; University of Missouri; LML Payment Systems (Vancouver BC); Deloitte & Touche Consulting and NetStar Corporation's ***Electronic Checks at the Point of Sale***; and MoveMoney.com, Inc. since January 1999.

The author's check predications and research have been requested for use by TeleCheck Services Inc., International Check Payments, Deluxe Check Printers (SCAN division), Federal Reserve Bank of Philadelphia, Digital Check Corporation, LML Payment Systems, Check Payment Systems Association, US Bank, and has been placed online for the corporate use of NCR Canada and NCR Scotland.

The check research is also cited in ***Short-Term Financial Management: Text and Cases*** by Terry S. Maness and John T. Zietlow (The Dryden Press), a textbook used in universities as a primary text for finance students.

Quote Sources

Quotes in the boxes on page 3, 4, and 5.

Changing Times: The Kiplinger Magazine, October 1975, pp 6-8.

Statement by George W. Mitchell, Vice Chairman, Board of Governors of the Federal Reserve System, before the subcommittee on Bank supervision and Insurance of the Committee on Banking and Currency, U.S. House of Representatives, November 26, 1973.

Sender, Isabelle, "Check Truncation Tempts Retailers," ***Chain Store Age Magazine***, May 1998,

About the Author........

Paul H. Green

Paul Green is Editor-In-Chief of ***The Green Sheet*** and ***GSQ: The Payment Systems Quarterly***, and is Chief Executive Officer of CrossCheck, Inc., the nation's largest independently owned check guarantee company. He is CEO of Concepts, Inc., a leading computer and Internet service company; and CEO/Founder of American Marketing Corporation (AMCOR), the nation's first bankcard Independent Sales Organization. Paul was previously president of Telecredit Check Services, Inc., prior to its acquisition by Equifax, and was responsible for that company's 300 million to 3 billion dollars a year growth.

Paul's other books include ***Good Selling!*** a tool for sales professionals offering sales training, tips, and motivation. This book outlines the basics from Getting Organized to Presentations and Closing. It has practical advice for beginners and reminders for those who have been selling for some time.

Paul Green holds a BA degree in Accounting and Computer Science, an MBA, and has been a Financial Executive Institute Member for over 20 years. Recently, he was awarded the Republican Senatorial Medal of Freedom, "The highest honor the Republican members of the U.S. Senate can bestow." Paul is a noted lecturer, an acclaimed artist and art collector, an amateur classicist and biblical historian, an avid outdoorsman and world-class explorer. Paul has been happily married to his wife, Tischa, for 32 years.

About The Green Sheet

In 1983, after first founding AMCOR, Paul Green recognized there was a rapidly growing, national sales force that needed training and motivation. Thus, ***The Green Sheet***, his biweekly motivational newsletter with "actionable advice" for those in the Financial Services Industry, was born. Over the last 16 years, ***The Green Sheet*** has been evolving with the ISO and is now the only publication for the Financial Services Industry published simultaneously on the Internet and paper.

Features in ***The Green Sheet*** include business opportunities, information resources, evolving technologies, banking and legal changes, and government issues. The newsletter features The Resource Guide, an advertising section that includes contact information for companies and services vital to the Financial Services industry. ***The Green Sheet*** also offers sales appropriate articles such as selling tips and motivational information, which continue to be the highest rated information from the Sales Professional's perspective. To further service the ISO, all articles are permanently archived and can be accessed via The Green Sheet's web site.

In 1995 The Green Sheet became its own independent publishing company, The Green Sheet, Inc., which now publishes the 32-page newsletter, ***The Green Sheet***, ***GSQ: The Payment Systems Quarterly*** magazine, and The Green Sheet On-Line (www.greensheet.com). In 1999 The Green Sheet, Inc. began publishing reference books for the Financial Services Industry. ***Good Selling!***, a primer for Independant Sales Agents has sold more than 10,000 copies in its first six months. These publications, whether in print or electronic form, are dedicated to serving as a forum where ISOs receive bias-free, timely information relevant to the rapidly expanding financial services market. The Green Sheet, Inc. provides data applicable to all aspects of the market including check verification and guarantee, bankcard and ATM services, debit, credit, EFT, ECP, and Internet commerce.

THE GREEN SHEET, INC.

Do you subscribe to *The Green Sheet?*

1st-year Free subscriptions available for

The Green Sheet & **GSQ**.

Contact us at:

800-757-4441

grnsht@aol.com

www.greensheet.com

P.O. Box 6008

Petaluma, CA 94955-6008